CW00749791

When

You

Hear

Meow

By

Alec Gould

© 2022 by Alec Gould All rights reserved. Copyright under Berne Copyright Convention, Universal Copyright Convention, and Pan-American Copyright Convention. No part of this book may be reproduced, stored in a retrieval system, or transmitted in any form, or by any means, electronic, mechanical, photocopying, recording or otherwise, without prior permission of the author.

A JumpingCatPublication

ISBN 978-1-7364564-2-2

More great books to read, by Alec Gould:

- **We Really Need To Laugh**
- **Ploop**
- **Ted-D's Happy, Sad, Birthday Day**
- **Eternal Sin – The L.A. Story**
- **Kruser's Point of View**

Www.AlecGould.com

Don liked his Yorkies, his Poms.

Then Gloria came into his life.

She brought Alec-the-Cat. . .

Contents

I
Story Telling

As the winds howled outside the window, the wintery mix came down as if we were in a snow globe. I pet the kitties upon my lap. I look at the other two, one curled upon my legs, the other between my waist and the arm of the chair. A symphony of purring in awe of their being. Me? I felt like Santa there in the living room waiting for Gloria to arrive home. Thankfully, she didn't work too far away, the roads being covered in this white stuff some people find nice. Well, OK, maybe from inside your home, not having to go anywhere. But other than that, not now, not as this old man sitting here covered in cat hair. At least I still have my youthful, warped humor to keep me entertained. And these fur balls that I love so much: Nellie, Boo-Boo, Yogi, and Marbles.

Purring and curled up in that way only kittens can do without getting hurt, they looked at me with a want for knowledge. I could see it through the windows to their souls, they knew it themselves, but were too young yet to know how to put their charm to use.

"So, you all want to know why you are here? Yes. Yes. I see that look. So gosh darn cute you all are, how can I not resist?" Their ears perked up at the sound of my voice, or was it the sound outside the window? A plow made a futile pass to clear the snow, more of which was to come in the night. I sipped my coffee and gave Nellie a belly rub, the others looking on in anticipation.

They knew I always had a story to tell, and their ears were at attention. With the now quiet from the street and the fireplace going, it was indeed a good day for a story. I cleared my throat in preparedness of giving these little ones a bit o' history of before their time. Of what had been and of what is now.

"My buddies," I began, clearing my throat one more time. "My buddies, let me tell you a story of long ago when your mother moved in with me. Now, we had known each other for many moons but had never lived together so this was all new for each of us. Yes, we loved one another but when people move in together, you learn different quirks about the other, some of which may question your mind about what you just did. Maybe you would have been better off living alone. But we had a love such as the seashore and the sea. Complementing each other in all we did. We figured it to only become better."

*****

"Honey, I'm home." I heard her voice enter through the open shop door, floating on the fall air like a gently released leaf.

"I'm in the machine room," I called back over my shoulder, busy working on a project. "Glad you're home. Did you have a good day?"

Giving her a hug and a kiss before she could answer, she replied that the day was beginning to get better. I had to agree. After three marriages between us consisting of three children – all girls, three dogs and multiple inside and outside cats, we had finally crossed the bridge to realizing our dream. The dream of spending our life together. Still, something seemed amiss.

"What's wrong, Love?" I asked her.

"Nothing's wrong. Why do you ask?"

"I see it in your eyes. Missing your daughter?"

"Well, yes. I know it has only been a week since we helped her move into her dorm room but that isn't the issue."

"Let's go outside and sit on the swing." I suggested. "I'll grab another beer and we can take our time talking. Would you like something to drink? I might have a soda in the old beer fridge."

"No thanks. I'm good."

Sitting on the swing, Gloria's feet dangling just above the lawn, tippy toes within her favorite pair of black shoes getting new scuffs, rocking us back and forth. Me relaxing to the rhythm. Noticing the far off look in her eyes, I asked the same question as before, "What's wrong, Love?"

"You're going to think I'm crazy. But you know how I have always had cats around in my life. Even back when you and I first met I had cats. My gosh, that was over forty years ago," she gasped.

I laughed, "That's a lot of cats."

Gloria nodded with a smile, blushing. "Yes, it is." She laughed.

"Yes, I remember. Even when you were on the CB radio, I remember your handle being "The Cat Lady." You always liked cats, that's for sure. Are you missing them out at the old farmhouse?"

"Yes." A tear appeared in her eye closest to me. Then I noticed a tear in the other eye as she turned towards me. She reached out and brought my hand into hers, clasping it tenderly. "Do you think I could bring one of the cats here to live with us?"

"One cat?" I jokingly asked. "How could you possibly pick out just one cat out of, what, thirty or so that you have out there?"

"Well, I would only be choosing an inside cat. That limits the amount to choose from. Plus, it would be a female, because, well, males tend to spray. And we do not want that in our house, do we?"

"So true. I haven't worked on this house for all these years only to have it ruined by a cat."

"So?"

"So what?" I asked, the smile lines in my face increasing.

"Oh, Honey, thank you!" She gave me a giant hug and then finished it off with another, and a kiss.

"Just hold on now. Not so quick, Love. I didn't quite say yes yet." She backed away, sadness replacing the tears in her eyes.

"What? Do they need to pay rent, too?"

"They?"

"Well, I meant only one, it just came out as they."

"No, "they" do not need to pay rent." I laughed. "But if "they" mess up, claw the woodwork, shred the furniture, pee on the carpet, or any other thing that would make this house a wreck, then "they" will be going back out to the farmhouse. Can you agree to that?"

"I understand, Honey. This is not a lion's den; this is our home. So, one cat, female, tomorrow?" Gloria asked with glee in her voice.

"I guess. Now, I don't want an angry cat, to which I am sure all your cats are full of love, but I remember a time when I was young, and a friend of mine and I came across a cat in an old chicken coop. I attempted to reach out to take it in my arms. Next thing I knew, it lashed out at me and opened the palm of my hand. Blood, my blood, spraying all over."

"No worries. As you said, and it is true, all my cats are full of love."

"OK then. So, do you have an idea which one is going to have the opportunity to be lucky enough to live with us?"

"Yes." Gloria beamed a wide smile. "Alec." She was so happy, I thought she sang his name. His???

"Hold it, I thought we agreed upon a female cat."

"Alec is a female. What can I say, my daughter named her." Gloria giggled. She looked so gosh darn cute doing it, too.

"Alrighty. Alec-the-Cat will be given the chance to live with us. But if she messes up, you know I wouldn't want to hurt your feelings, but Alec will have to be evicted. No ands, ifs, or buts. OK?"

Again, I swear Gloria was singing. "OK."

"You know, I really don't understand the idea behind having a cat. At least, not in town unless you've got problems with mice. Out on the farms I can see having them, but here? In a house without mice?"

Gloria looked at me as if I did not understand something that everyone should know. "They're magical. If you look into their eyes, you can see it. And" she paused here looking at me with concern. "And, if you really believe, they will talk. Just like a person, but more angelic."

"I thought you had quit drinking, but I must have been mistaken."

"It's true. If you give it time, if you really believe, you will understand."

"OK," I replied. Inside my head I was beginning to have doubts about this cat living here...and Gloria for that matter.

"All I know is that when I was growing up, we had two cats. Penny and Sassy. Neither of them talked, nor did much. Still, my ma loved them. They kept her company she would say to us kids. All I ever remember is her cleaning their litter box and running away from us kids."

"You kids probably scared them. They don't want to be scared; they want to be loved. No different than any other living creature."

"I suppose, but either way, if a cat will make this house feel more like a home for you, My Love, so be it. I just want you to be happy."

"Thanks Honey. I love you!" And with that, she danced into the house.

Me? I tossed the empty can into the recyclables and gave a pardon to another from the beer fridge. Time to get a project done. TGIF!

With that, I turned on the old stereo and cranked up Earl Thomas Conley's version of "Finally Friday". I finished my beer before the song was done and went to retrieve another. "Geez, these cans are getting smaller." I laughed.

My mind drifted back to the conversation out on the swing. Cats. Magical? My gosh, did I really hear her say that? Or did I drink a few more beers than I realize before she got home?

Either way, a cat? I had been a dog person for the past fifteen years. Granted, dogs not much bigger than some cats, but dogs all the same. Yorkies and Poms, of which I enjoyed the Poms more. Less yippee, more fun. Oh, how I missed Bandit. That little black and white puff ball. No doubt, he was the most handsome of Poms.

That little guy hung outside as much as I did. Didn't matter if I was cutting tree limbs or working on an old motorcycle, he was always there. He was the reason I would take a break at times.

I'd be working on some project, and he'd come into the shop, sit down and look up at me. That was all it took. "Alright buddy," I would say with a smile. "I take it, it's time to play a bit?"

He would run circles in front of me, stop with a jolt, put his front paws on my knees and bark happily. After all that, he would run outside, pick up a toy for me to throw and … oh, how I miss him. If I hadn't been so nice in the divorce, he'd still be here. Yet, she was the one who wanted to get a dog. Damn heart of mine! I hope Bandit is doing well.

Unblurring my vision, reality returned. Get rid of those memories now, Don, and get to work. Nothing is going to change not having Bandit here. At least you were able to spend some good time with him. Now, get rid of that empty can, grab a fresh beer, and get to work. There's sandblasting that needs to get finished tonight.

II
WE Have a Cat

The morning greeted me with one heck of a headache. Yet, the sun was out, the sky was blue, and it was Saturday. No work this weekend for either of us. Headache or no headache, it was great to be alive. Saturday meant we could do whatever we wanted to; go out to eat, get on Paradise and go for a ride, or...

"What? Who is, or what is, a Paradise you ask?" The kitties on my lap looked up at me as if that was what they were asking.

"Well, my feline friends, let me tell you. A Paradise was your momma's and my first Harley Davidson motorcycle. It was a Sportster, a small bike, especially for the two of us. Then again, we were both thinner back then. We named it Paradise because it got us away from all the stresses life seemed to have in store for us during that time. But, when we would take that key out of my pocket, we had the key to Paradise and all our stress would leave us, at least for the time we were riding." Boo-boo curled her head under her sister Marbles and the other two purred. Apparently, they were satisfied with my explanation. I continued the story...

As I was saying, it was the weekend and Gloria and I could do whatever we wished for these two days.

Hearing Gloria yawn in the bedroom, I thought she may be waking so I walked in and asked, "Hey, Love, what's up for today? Do you wish for me to make some omelets, or do you want to go out and eat?"

"What do you mean, what's up for today? Today I get to go and bring Alec home. And yes, num, num, omelets sound good, but let us go out to eat, ok?

That way I won't have any dishes and it will be more relaxing. Plus, I can spend some quality time with Alec to help her get used to her new home."

"That sounds like a good plan, Love. I'll go have a cup of coffee outside and wait for you to get ready. No rush."

"Good thing. I don't know if Kayla will be up yet, but I'll leave her a message that Alec will be coming to live with us."

"Yeah, she should know since she is the one that named him. I mean, her." It was going to take some time to get used to this name. Then again, Alec could be shortened from Alexandria. Yes, that is what I will think. I got myself a cup of coffee and went outside to enjoy the music of the birds.

Not being one that can sit for a long time, after a few sips of go-go juice I got up from the swing and paced the yard, only to find myself picking up the empty cans from the night before. "I really should buy stock in beer," I thought.

Back on the swing, I watched a beautiful male cardinal at one of the feeders. Joining him was a black-capped chickadee.

The breeze brought in a smell of freshness as a bunny hopped across the lawn, heading for the safety of the wood pile. He knew there was a hawk in the area and he was not going to be dinner, not if he could help it.

I am not one for getting up early for work but to come outside to the back yard and watch nature, to listen to the birds, that I did not mind. I brought the coffee cup to my lips, tipped my head back for that last bit and felt a drop of rain.

How can this be, the sky is clear? I was about to put my hand up to wipe away the wetness when Gloria yelled from the driveway, "Stop" and started laughing.

"What?" I asked.

"A bird just pooped on your head," she replied, laughing harder. "I'll go get some paper towels."

"Great, the Bird of Paradise just visited me, and this is what it left? I prefer it to go by the neighbor next time."

On the way to the diner, Gloria stated that maybe the Bird of Paradise was just warming up, maybe it will be more prosperous next time. I should just be patient.

"Yeah, well, why not. I've sat around being patient all these past years just to be crapped on, I guess I can do it a wee bit longer. With any luck, it'll be a Sandhill Crane".

Amidst our laughter, Gloria stated, "One must be positive now, Honey. P-O-S-I-T-I-V-E. If we are always negative, we will never get anywhere."

"True dat, My Love. True dat."

After breakfast Gloria took me home. Now that we were becoming feline parents, she had to go to the big box store to purchase some necessities. After stocking up there, she was off to the farmhouse to gather up Ms. Alec.

A few hours later found me hearing her van pull into the driveway, beeping the horn. Walking out of my shop I found her running towards me, smiling, her arms out to give me a bear hug.

"Alec is waiting to meet you, Honey."

I laughed a bit at her happiness. Not downplaying it, but very happy myself for seeing My Love this happy. It had been a rough year on both of us, with the divorces and getting situated with living together. Now? We have a cat. A cat? My gosh what was I thinking?

Gloria took me by the hand and led me to her van. Opening the side door, she pulled out a cat carrier and introduced me to this beautiful tuxedoed kitty cat. I was astounded by her poise. Alec simply looked up at the two of us, crouched down on her legs in this cage, un-enthused. I put my finger into the holes of her carrier and attempted to pet her.

"Hi there, Alec. So, you're going to live with us now, ey?" I tried to sound positive.

"Yes, she is," Gloria answered for Alec.

Apparently, I thought to myself, all that talk about cats being able to talk was bull. No kidding! I laughed to myself but didn't say anything to Gloria what I had thought. I mean, why?

Gloria continued, "I think she'll really like it here. She'll have the whole house to herself, no other kitties to battle for her dinner bowl or trying to go potty with the others around. Yes, I think she is really going to like it here."

"Well, Love," I said, interrupting her roll-on words. "keep in mind what I had said. If Alec here starts ruining the furniture or making a mess in our house, she goes. Understand?"

"Yes," Gloria lowered her head and then rebounded back up. "but she will be good. You'll see."

"Alright, Love, alright. I'll give you a hand getting the kitty supplies inside. You can bring in Alec."

Gloria didn't release Alec until I had brought in the food and kitty litter. And kitty toys. No doubt, Gloria was going to make sure that Alec-the-Cat had what she needed to be happy.

Bringing Alec into the living room, Gloria asked if I was ready to open the door of the pet carrier, to which I did. Alec took her good natured, possibly a bit in fear, time to step out of the carrier. She sniffed the air and looked behind her. Seeing only Gloria and myself, no other kitties around like she had been used to, she took a few more steps into the room, away from the refuge of her carrier.

"Now, Alec," I began. "I'm sure your mother told you, but I will repeat it. If you make any messes or start ruining the furniture, you will need to be returned to the farmhouse. Understand?"

Alec looked up at me, almost as if she understood what I was saying. While Gloria got her some food and her litter box ready, I picked her up and got a bit more acquainted. Surprisingly, Alec let me do so without a fuss, nor a hiss. So far, so good.

Gloria came back into the room stating we should show Alec where her food and litter box was going to be, now that things were ready in that area. I carried Alec into her new room. When we got in there, the first thing I did was to put her down inside her litter box. Alec sniffed around a bit, putting her paws into the litter, moving it a bit like a kid at the beach, turned around a few times while looking at me then... she surprised the heck out of me. She went to the bathroom, right there and then. I smiled, as did Gloria.

"See, I told you she's smart."

"I thought you said she was magical?"

Gloria smiled, "That too."

After supper that night, watching TV, I noticed Alec had not been in the room for some time. Gloria and I got up out of our seats and began to look all over, bedrooms, kitchen, bathroom; Alec was nowhere upstairs. We went down to the basement in panic mode. As we went downstairs, we continued to call out for Alec. No mews to be heard.

We checked in the family room first. Both of us on our knees checking beneath the chairs and couch. Not there. We then went into the washer and dryer area with the same amount of misfortune. Going into my downstairs work area, found us once again on our knees as we looked under the work benches. This time, we were lucky.

"Did you hear something, Honey?"

"No. Just the hot water heater kicking on."

"There, there it is again." Gloria called out Alec's name. "Are you OK, Alec?" She asked.

"Mew." Alec responded

"OK, that I heard this time," I said. I turned around, still on my knees, and looked in the middle shelf of the bench I was near. There she was, scared.

"Poor girl," I said.

Putting my hands in the space I petted her, trying to put her at ease.

"It's OK, Alec. Momma's right over there."

Gloria came over to show her face to Alec.

"Hi, Alec. Did you get scared and decide to hide?"

Alec looked at his momma but still stayed somewhat hidden within the shadows of the shelf.

"Daddy will get you out of there." Gloria moved so as I could reach in and get Alec, all the while Gloria kept talking calming words to keep Alec as relaxed as she could.

Reaching in, almost to the point of not being able to touch her, I was able to get ahold of her. Poor girl was so scared, I had to pull her out by her front legs. Yet, scared as she was, she didn't hiss, scratch, or bite me. I was surprised at all the fore mentioned.

"Alec is a mellow cat," Gloria said with pride. "She wouldn't hurt anyone."

"Well, that is a first for me. But I am very happy about that." I rubbed Alec's ear for a bit as she seemed to melt in my protective arms. "Oh, it's OK, Alec. New places to check out sometimes can scare us, don't they?"

Gloria looked at me smiling from ear to ear.

"What?" I asked.

"Nothing. Nothing at all." She replied. "Well, except, aren't you the gentle giant now? So, cats aren't that terrible to have, are they?"

"Well, the poor girl is scared. Cat or not, she doesn't know what is going on yet. She has a lot to learn in her new place."

"Her new place? Does that mean you have decided she can stay permanently now?"

"Time will tell, Love. Time will tell." I smiled. But, before I handed Alec over to Gloria I whispered in Alec's ear, "You do realize, if you were a dog this would not have happened."

Alec looked at me like, "You idiot. A dog would have crapped on the floor."

"Did you say something, Honey?"

"No. Nothing, Love." I presented Alec to Gloria's waiting arms.

As the three of us returned to the living room, Alec continued to be comforted while we watched TV The rest of that night Alec remained close to Gloria. New places. They can scare anyone. Even me.

As time passed, Alec seemed to have taken ownership of our house. We listened to her beckon call of when she was hungry, scratched her belly when she rolled over, and brushed her hair like she was a queen. The strange thing was, I did not mind. Alec was such a good girl.

Even though Alec was good, that Christmas I was told by Gloria that we should not put a tree up. That cats like to climb in them and each ornament is a toy waiting to be played with. I agreed. I mean, who needs the mess? Still...

After a late night out in the shop and a case of beer put into the recycling can, I awoke to the sound of boxes being pushed around in the kitchen. Gloria had gotten up early. It was 9:00 a.m. Real early.

Struggling to get dressed, my head again aching from the prior night's hydration, I finally managed to get myself into the kitchen to see what all the fuss was about.

"Good morning, Honey."

"Good morning, Love. What's with all the empty boxes?"

"I thought I would decorate a bit for Christmas. Just because we can't have a tree doesn't mean we can't decorate. I hope you don't mind?" I watched Alec jump into a box, then out, then into another. "She likes boxes. Actually, all kitties like boxes."

I just smiled, thinking to myself, finally. I finally obtained something I was always after in life. A woman who loves me as much as I love her and together, we were working towards the same goals. This one being the goal of having a home of love.

"Now, close your eyes Honey and I'll lead you into a surprise." With that she took my hand and led me around the corner into the living room. "OK, you can open them."

I was amazed. Simply amazed. While I was sleeping off a hangover, here is this little woman carrying these fragile, yet heavy, boxes up from the basement and making their contents into works of Christmas magic.

"This. This is beautiful, Love." I was in awe. Standing in the center of the living room I slowly turned, taking in all the beauty that surrounded me. The fireplace mantle with a Christmas village upon it, the top of the entertainment center giving a prominent spot for the nativity scene, a Christmas village with a motorcycle garage complimenting the town of Bethlehem. She even had ornaments hanging from hooks attached to the lamp shades.

"Wowza!"

"Thanks, Honey. I was hoping you would like it. I mean, even though we can't have a tree, that doesn't mean we can't decorate a bit, right?" She smiled that beautiful smile of hers.

I turned to face her, gave her a kiss and a big hug and found myself being brushed on the ankles. Looking down I spied Alec brushing against me, smiling. Now, how can that be? Only dogs know how to smile. Oh well, I couldn't blame her. Momma did very well in the decorating.

Kayla Kitten came home during college break and together, along with Gloria's uncle, we had a beautiful Christmas dinner. No Norman Rockwell dinner, but it was still a dinner amongst the best. We were healthy and happy. The best either of us had felt in many moons.

Since I did the cooking, Gloria volunteered to do the dishes. That was a "rule" we made prior to cohabitating together. It works out very well for us.

Gloria says washing dishes is relaxing for her and as for me, I was not going to take a chance on being in another relationship eating fast foods on a nightly basis. Not that we would have, but I really did want to do the cooking.

After dishes, Gloria visited with her daughter on the couch. Both with their laptops open but happy to be together. Again, finally, a family moment that would always remain in my memory. I went into the kitchen to get Eggnog and Christmas cookies for the two of them.

The next day I found myself putting together, of all things, a cat tower. I did as I was asked, but let me tell you, I never once put anything together for a dog. Still, I did it because Alec seemed to have earned it. No messes. No clawing of furniture. Good dog. I mean, cat.

"Well, that wasn't too bad now, was it?" I asked Alec. Yes, I found myself beginning to talk to her like she was a friend. How could I not? She was always around, attached to me for whatever reason, even when Gloria was out grocery shopping or at work.

Alec looked up at me from the floor near her Christmas gift, this "Tower of Power" as it would be called forever forward. She sniffed at the material, then watched for my expression as she went to scratch her nails upon it. When I didn't yell at her for doing so, she hunched her back as if she were a tuxedoed panther then she really dug her nails in.

"Apparently, you like?" I smiled at her and with that, she bounded up the steps to the top platform, put her front paws over the edge and looked over her kingdom like a Queen of the Jungle.

"So, you do approve?"

Alec turned her face towards me and squinted her eyes. "Now, you don't really understand what I am saying," taking a pause and continuing, "do you?" She squinted her eyes at me again.

"OK, I'm just going to say..." Alec opened her mouth as if she was going to finish my sentence but instead curled up and began her nap. My thought? I'm losing it.

After that day, Alec liked her tower of power so much, we would find her sleeping in the high perch like a leopard on the African landscape. Snoring.

I was working at a manufacturing company during this time and since it was Christmas, they shut down for two weeks. That part I liked. Two weeks of freedom. Priceless. Well, except for the beer I was able to down during this time, but Gloria always bought that with the groceries, so it really wasn't costing me anything.

I must admit the beer was going down extremely well, as there was a night or two where she would come out to the shop about eight o'clock and ask me if I had enough to get through the night or if she should go to the beer cave. Silly question. The answer was always no, so she found herself at the beer cave quite a bit. Until...

It didn't matter what day of the week it was, I always had time to have a beer or ten. I called it my family tradition; others called it a problem. The only problem I found with it was I either came close to running out of beer or I had to piss a lot.

When I was out on the bike, I limited myself to two beers. At home? No limit. I mean, hey, I wasn't driving anywhere, I liked the music and for the patrons there in my shop, it was only me most of the time who I didn't mind all that much. The times Gloria came out, I always enjoyed. I'm not sure she did most times, but I did.

It didn't matter if we were simply talking or if I was making a move on her, I enjoyed the time spent together. Years later I began to understand why she would not have liked those times, even when we were simply talking. I must not have made a lot of sense then. Why do I say that? Because I started to write great ideas down on pieces of paper so as to remember them the next day. I always found out the following day they were never great ideas. Guess I am no Prince or Bowie.

Now, to get back to the drinking. I never had a temper when I drank but I would do stupid and sometimes funny things. I would never drink on New Year's Eve which was unusual. Then again, in my early twenties I never went out on Halloween or New Year's Eve. Must have stayed with me.

Today was Saturday and I had off work, again, a rare thing. So, it was out to the shop to get some projects done and a lot more drinking. Gloria was in the house watching TV and enjoying her time with Alec. I had grilled out brats earlier so supper and dishes were done. Time to relax.

Saturday night always found us enjoying SNL- Saturday Night Live – together. Her on the couch with Alec purring and myself in my chair, legs up. Both of us with a bowl of ice cream; chocolate chip mint. MMM.

***

Tightening the nut on the new exhaust system for the bike, I looked up at the clock on the microwave in the shop. 10:28 p.m.

"Crap!" I yelled out loud. Then continuing in my head, "I hate missing the monologue on SNL, lately that is the best part of the show. Well, that and "Weekend Update.""

I hurried to shut the lights off and lock up the shop. Running into the house, I got irate. There, on the couch, lie Gloria. No ice cream in sight and the TV was not even on.

"What the hell, Love? Where's the ice cream, why isn't the TV on?"

"I didn't know you were coming in." she sounded scared.

"I always come in for SNL. That is the only time you and I really spend time together, where we can laugh and relax instead of always working on something." I was disgusted.

Picking Alec up from her legs, she fumbled with the TV controls, stating she would get the ice cream.

SNL appeared on the TV as she hurried toward the kitchen.

"Don't worry about the ice cream now, Love. You'll miss the monologue."

"It doesn't matter," she replied. "We always have ice cream now and I should had known better."

"Love ---" I stopped talking. I knew she was both hurt and upset. What really hurt was she was upset with me, and I couldn't blame her. She meant the world to me, and this is how I treat her? RRRRRR!

Alec looked up at me, shook her head as if, "What in the world is wrong with you? You keep this up and you are going to find yourself alone."

Gloria came back as the monologue finished and a commercial came on to take its place. Handing me a bowl of ice cream, I asked her where hers was.

"There wasn't much left, so I gave it to you."

"We can split it, Love."

"No, I don't want any."

I knew I should just shut up. I felt like dying then and there. I'm a fool.

I woke up about eleven the next morning, having gone back out to the shop to finish putting the new exhaust on the bike. Gloria wasn't in bed, but then again, she usually got up before me and I would find her sitting in her chair in the living room. Not today. Today, I only found Alec in the chair.

"Where's Momma, Alec?"

Alec looked at me like, "You fool. I told you you were pushing the limits, but you didn't hear me. What is wrong with you?"

I went into the kitchen.

I called downstairs for her.

Only silence answered.

I turned towards the coffee pot.

I noticed a piece of paper near my cup. . .

"Honey, I can't do this anymore. Your drinking is getting worse. It seems that it is more important to you than me. I had enough of this type of living with my dad, I am not going to go through it again with you. I took the few things I had moved in with, but Alec needs to stay with you. She has become fond of you, and I believe, in time, you will understand her better. Right now, I am moving in with a girlfriend. Call only if you quit your drinking. Otherwise, maybe down the line, I might call but only time will tell. You've broke my heart. Yet, I still love you. G"

I was in disbelief. How could she move out like this? I wasn't a mean drunk. I didn't drink and drive, much. I was faithful to her. I've been told I am funny when I drink, that I make people laugh. So, I enjoyed drinking, so what?

I looked down at Alec brushing against my leg. Picking her up, I held her close to me, hearing her purr, and left my heart break. In my pain, I thought I heard a voice. Not an imagined voice, but one which came from Alec. It was as if I heard her say, "I tried to warn you. To make you aware. Yet, you simply opened another beer and thought things would be alright. Well, here we are. You. And me. Me with the wet hair." Of course, I did not hear her speak those words. Instead, I heard Alec sneeze. I reached into my pocket for a handkerchief and proceeded to wipe her nose.

III
Bonding

The next days were torture on me. I took some vacation and sat in my office at home, staring out the window and petting Alec. I didn't type a single word in the book in progress, even though I was almost done writing it. I knew I was in depression mode. It wasn't easy on either one of us. Hell, I didn't even know what to feed her. I, of course, knew where Gloria worked but Gloria didn't tell me where she had gone to stay. I knew her well enough that meant "stay away, do not contact."

Knowing all the problems I had caused with my drinking and that she was serious about me quitting the life of an alcoholic, I was not going to give her any more reason to not want to come back to me. We had been separated in life for too many years. Now that we were together, both of us divorced from the evils within our old lives, I wanted to make everything better. I wanted to show her that my love for her meant more to me than another beer. But, oh, how I loved my beer. The nectar of the God's sent in an aluminum can. MMM, that good, ol', dark, craft beer. MMM MM! But, due to my irresponsibility in this field, I knew I had to quit. No different than when I quit smoking. Only then it was because I was afraid. Afraid I was going to die since I had issues with breathing. This time, if I did not quit the drinking, I was going to have issues with living; living my life without my one true love to share it with me.

The breeze came in the open window, smelling cool and fresh. Spring. Beautiful in its way of showing how the world is reborn. I never really cared for winter; spring gave me hope. Staring out the window herself, Alec enjoyed me petting her. As she looked up at me, I noticed some gunk in her eye.

"Is that better?" I asked her as I put the handkerchief back in my pocket.

She squinted, taking a paw to rub the corner of her eye. She just gave me a stare.

"Yes, you do seem to have me at your beckon call now, doesn't it?" I smiled at her. "Feeding and petting you most of the day until you decide that it is enough. Cleaning out that litter box of yours which, by the way, I am so very happy you use that and don't make a mess. You know? You seem to be growing on me. I've never known a cat to be like you, almost dog-like; but easier. I don't have to get up in the middle of the night to take you out. I like that."

I continued to pet Alec as she laid on my lap. The breeze came in the window again, fresh as the day. Leaning back in the chair, I dozed. Alec did the same.

Since I did not have much vacation left, I found myself going back to work sooner than I wanted to. It wasn't easy, but in hindsight, I found it to be of benefit to myself. Yet, when I went to work, I found I was missing Alec as much as I was missing Gloria. How could that be?

Get this. I think she might be getting attached to me too. When I pull out of the drive to go to work, I see her in the kitchen window. She would take her paw to open the curtains, squeeze in between the left and right and watch me get into my truck.

The first time I noticed her doing this, I was in disbelief. I put my window down and waved at her which, in return, she would blink her eyes in a fashion that I took to say, "I'll miss you. Hurry home, Daddy. I love you."

Yes, I am getting worried. About what? Me. I think I am losing it.

Yet, I swear that Alec is part dog. I mean, she greets me at the door each night I get home from work. She doesn't do it during the day when I might go in the back yard to feed the birds or work in the shop, but every night when I come home, she is there to greet me, rolling on her back, legs up in the air; waiting for a belly rub to which, of course, she gets. How could I not?

Since I wasn't that knowledgeable about cats, I began to do some research. I knew they ate, pooped, scratched furniture, and meowed. Oh, and shed a lot of hair. Except, Alec-the-Cat did not do all of these things in which I had thought I knew so well. Thankfully, she did not scratch the furniture. As for the hair she lost? I wished I could salvage it for my own scalp. Alas, it was not possible.

I was relieved that she did not ruin the furniture, especially since she had her claws. Gloria told me that every cat should have their claws because if they ever got out of the house, they could still protect themselves and get away from danger. Without them they could not climb trees or lash out. That makes sense.

The one thing I was surprised to learn though was cats, just like dogs, look forward to their humans coming home after being gone all day at work. Why? Well, think about when we are home all day, every day, not going anywhere. We tend to get a little bored and need something to liven us up such as TV or reading a good book. Cats or dogs? Other than watching out the window for critters to scamper by, they are pretty much dependent upon us for their foods and waters being changed. Cleaning out their litter box or, in the case of doggies, taking them outside to go potty and for their walks. We are their lives. Their entertainment. So, I began to change it up a bit when I would get home.

Instead of simply taking my jacket and shoes off then rubbing Alec's belly for a few seconds while saying, "Good girl" I would get myself sat on the basement steps and be eye level with her, talking one-on-one while she purred and rubbed against my offering hand for a belly rub. She ate it up and so did I. This became our ritual. Daddy and Alec-the-Cat's bonding time. I think she enjoyed it as much as I did. Again, I never would have thought a cat to behave such as she did. I liked that!

Those first couple of weeks without Gloria were pure hell on me and Alec. Not that they were great later, but one becomes used to how their situation is. In my case, it was better than it had been, but not as great as when Gloria was living with me.

After supper, Alec would relax with me in my chair to watch a bit of TV as I had a cup of coffee. She'd lay there in my lap, belly warm from all the rubbing she kept me busy doing, and purring. She was cool. Again, I had little dogs before and never would have guessed a cat could be so neat.

A comedy or two later, Alec would join me in the office where I would get to writing more in the new novel, a novel that I had been working on for months. As all writers, I thought this novel was going to be the breaking point where I would never have to go to work for someone else again. Reality being as truthful and heartless as it is, reminded me my marketing skills sucked.

I had a few books out and they were selling well through the major book venues but not at a pace where I could count on the sales as positive, always there, income. Still, I persisted.

Alec would follow me into the office, and we would begin our ritual of her and me clawing at the scratching post for wisdom. It seemed as if she liked the attention. She would look at me with those green kitty eyes and squint, almost as if she were saying, "You're doing OK for not being drunk all the time. I'm beginning to get attached to you." I would then sit at the desk, Alec behind me, on top of my chair, behind my head doing the editing, so it seemed. She kept me company. I liked it, she liked it. My apologies. Apologies for digressing these past couple pages...

As I came out of my slumber, I heard a noise. At first, I thought I was in bed with Gloria and that she was snoring but this wasn't a snore. Beginning to awaken a bit more, my ears getting tuned in, it finally came to me. That's a purr. Looking down at Alec, still in my lap, apparently content, she purred. Awww.

Again, she purred, this time loud. WOW!

I had to record this on my phone. She is so cool!

As I soon found out, timing is everything. No sooner than I recorded her purring, the timer on my phone began playing, reminding me it was time to write. Alec looked up at me from her relaxed state as if, "What is with all that noise? I am trying to snooze here."

Leaving the reminder play on the phone, I took Alec in my arms. Looking at her as I held her in my arms, I said, "Let's dance, buddy" and with that, we had our first dance. I must confess, this was a bit strange, if not weird. Dancing with one's cat? I would not have given it a thought if I was drinking, because even then, I would not have danced with a cat. Jeez! I put Alec down as the song ended, her looking up at me like I was losing it. Yet, all she did was blink her eyes at me, like she was Endora on that Bewitched show of the sixties.

The rest of the night, as I typed on the ol' keyboard, she lay in my lap, purring. As I finished putting the final words into the document before me, I sat back, leaving out a sigh. Looking at what I had written and deciding if it were good or not, I felt Alec on my head.

"What are you doing there, buddy?" I wanted to move around to check her out but whatever she was doing felt great. I sat back in my chair to so-call, take it all in.

Apparently, Alec had felt the aura of stress that enveloped my being and thought I needed a head massage for that was almost what you could say she was doing. Or at least I hope she was, since I had already fed her.

Feeling the stress release its grasp from me, Alec continued gnawing my head. All I could do was lean back in my chair and go "Ahhhh." While doing so, my mind cleared itself, releasing its dopamine, filling my entirety with a feeling of goodness.

"How did she know I was stressed out? Does she feel the external energies as I do myself? Are cats prone to being empaths? I did not have the answers, but something told me she did, but she wasn't talking." All I could do was sit back and enjoy.

The next morning I awoke to the thump of Alec jumping off the bed and running towards the kitchen. That's when I heard keys. Gloria? It must be. Why else would Alec run towards an unknown sound?

"Gloria?" I asked as I walked to the kitchen.

"Yes, it's me. I thought I would see how you were waking up in the mornings."

"What do you mean, Love?"

"Well, you were always hung over so I just wanted to see if you were trying to quit the drinking or if things were the same with you."

"I haven't had a drink since you left me the note." She followed my gaze, her note still where she put it on the counter. Right next to the last beer I drank.

"You haven't?"

"Your love means the world to me. I do not want to take a chance anymore and lose it for good."

She smiled at Alec. Alec rubbed against Gloria's legs. "Meow."

"Is Daddy telling the truth, Alec?"

Alec looked up at Gloria. "Yes, Daddy hasn't had a drop of alcohol at all, Momma. He really missed you."

I thought I was losing it. Was Gloria really in the kitchen? Did Alec really talk? Did I really quit drinking or was I just hallucinating after another night of drunkenness?

"Is that so, Alec?"

Alec nodded in response. "He loves you, Momma. Now, can I have a potato chip? I miss my potato chip time with you."

"Of course, you can, Alec. In just a moment though. Let us take care of Daddy first."

Lying me down in bed, Gloria said, "I told you kitties are magical."

I couldn't say anything. Laying there, staring at the ceiling fan go around in circles. I was simply bewildered.

Alec, sitting on my chest, looked me in the eyes and said, "Meow."

IV
Magic Time

After all the "excitement" I dozed off and the next thing I knew, it was almost noon. Gloria had run to the local fast-food place to get us something to eat. And Alec? Well, she was lying next to me in bed, watching me with those magical green eyes, and purring fondly.

"It took you awhile. For a bit, I wasn't sure if Momma was correct in what she seen in you. Yup, you surprised me when you finally heard me talking. Yup, took a bit. Geez!" Then she laughed! At me!

"You were surprised at me? I still think I'm dreaming. Or maybe I am still drinking? Or maybe I'm trying something different and I'm ---."

"No, you are sane. You are not drunk. You are not stoned. You have finally crossed over the line to keeping a clear mind and open ears. There are many people who can hear us cats talk. There are also many people who will never hear us talk. Those are the non-believers. The ones that don't believe in anything as magic. Mmph! If you ask a lot of cats what they think, they will tell you the same thing I would. We are surprised a lot of people can manage without us."

I sat there in disbelief. "Why couldn't I hear you before?"

"You were clouding your vision and ears with alcohol. Now, don't think of me as saying that alcohol is bad. Just as anything else in life, moderation is a great habit to have. You did not have that. All you wanted was another beer.

And then another and another and another."

"I know. I don't know why, but I just needed the buzz."

"Now, now. You don't need to lie to me. You forget, all those days you couldn't hear me, I was listening to you. Listening and watching you. You were trying to kill yourself, weren't you? I saw it in your eyes. It didn't matter what day it was or how the weather was or even how much Momma loved you. You simply had had it with life. The buzz would get going and you would pass it up with a few more beers."

"Now, Alec, that's a bit rough, don't cha think?" I leaned up on my elbow and looked at Alec in amazement that this was really happening.

"Not at all, Daddy. You don't mind me calling you Daddy, do you?" I shook my head no. Alec continued, "No, not a bit rough. Not at all. Remember that night you came into the house all drunk and you fell on the floor in the bathroom? Before that all took place, didn't you have a nice buzz when you took out the garbage that night?"

"Yes, come to think of it, I did."

"So, why didn't you come in the house after you had the garbage taken out to the road? Momma was inside waiting for you to spend time with her."

"I don't know."

"Well, I believe I do. You didn't want to live, but you didn't understand why. Even with Momma giving her all in this household, her love to you and only you and yet, you still wanted to die. Instead, I watched you go back out to the garage for another fifteen minutes and downed as much moonshine as you could, then you stumbled back into the house and made Momma worry sick because she didn't know what she could do for you. Do you remember that?"

"Yes, I do. I remember she got me to bed. Then she told me she had to get food in my belly to try and soak up what I had consumed."

"Yes. Yes, she did all that. For you. That is how much she loves you. So, I hope you never touch a drop of alcohol again. You've seen that video by Ozzie Osbourne, Under the Graveyard?"

I nodded that I had.

"Well, that video could had been made about how you were living. Please, for the sake of love in this house, do not drink anymore. We all love you. Now, it is time for you to love yourself. Got it?"

"Got it." I couldn't believe I was talking to, wait, no, with a cat. And she was making perfect sense! Alec laid on her back, paws in the air and said, "Now, if you don't mind, please rub my belly. A-hum, oh yes, purrrrr."

I did as I was asked. How could I not?

***

Gloria moved back in; the beer moved out to the trash. A cruel, sorrowful death indeed, but I had to make sure it was gone. Since I did pour each one out in the garden, the dirt crawlers could have had a party down below. As for that new still I bought, it makes a nice decoration in my office. Unused.

The money Gloria was using to buy my beer was now being used for a hobby she had always wanted to get involved with, gem collecting. As time passed, and the boxes of gems began arriving from all over the states, she found there were other items besides gems available from these people. Sometimes she would buy dragons made of different composites. Other times it might be a miniature kitty made of something unique. One time she bought a skeletal looking dragon. When that arrived, she had to call us into the kitchen to see.

"What is that?" I asked.

"Just something a bit different. I thought you would get a kick out of it."

"It is different but cool looking. I just never thought of you buying something that was all bones." I laughed a bit to which Alec jumped out of my arms and onto the kitchen table where this item stood.

"I think he is the coolest looking dragon I have ever seen." She began to rub her body against him. "He feels so good. Even for a little creature such as he is."

"What are you going to name him, Love?" I asked.

"I don't know. We will give it a little time and see what it feels like to be named."

"Well, from the looks of how Alec is acting with him, I believe she might already have a name in mind. Do you, Alec?"

We both looked at Alec and without a blink of an eye, she replied, "Rubs. I believe he should be known as Rubs. Rubs, The Great Protector." With that, Rubs had now joined our little family.

The days and weeks passed nicely. Work still sucked and book sales weren't doing as great as I needed. As for Gloria, her job was keeping her so busy that she was going in on weekends. That is how dedicated a person she is. As for Alec? She and I were getting along rather well. I had grown to love her as much as any dog I had ever had. Yet, when I told her that, she would say "You better." She thought rather highly of herself, but what had I expected? She's a cat. She's a good girl.

With the trees in their gowns of green and the birds and bunnies in family ways, the month changed on the calendar to Gloria's birthday. I did not want to take a chance on missing out on getting her a gift on time, so I ordered a special gift about five weeks prior. I really hoped she would like it. Alec told me she would.

Kayla Kitten was coming over Saturday to help celebrate her mom's birthday with us -yes, she could hear Alec-the-Cat, too. We were going to have a mid-afternoon dinner with a homemade cake after a cookout. It would be good.

Gloria slept in that morning while I worked on mowing and trimming the yard. It felt good to finally be working on the grass after all the snow this past winter. Much nicer outside, no heavy jacket nor boots. No hangovers.

Kayla came over about 1:00 p.m. so I cooked dinner on the grill while Alec su-purr-vised from the office window. "You're doing well there, Daddy-O. Although I'm not sure I would leave them on that side much longer. Yes, I would turn those brats over now before they burn. How would that look on Momma's birthday? Burned brats don't go too well with homemade cake and frosting I hear." She then laughed. She really thought she had a great sense of humor, and I must admit, at times she did.

***

"Touch him right behind his ears, go ahead. Now, touch his right paw." Gloria did as Alec had instructed, but she nor I or Kayla had any idea what this was about. "No, no, his other right paw, Momma."

"I'm getting nervous, Alec. OK, his right paw. Now what?" Gloria asked.

I had gotten Gloria a teddy bear for her birthday and for whatever reason, Alec was telling us how to take care of him. So, we did as we were told, although none of this made sense. Then, it happened.

"Now, wiggle his left foot." Gloria wiggled the teddy bear's left foot. "OK, get ready."

We looked at Alec. "Ready for what?" we asked.

"Why, ready for the surprise."

We looked at Alec and noticed she was staring in deep concentration towards the teddy bear; we followed suit.

Before us, we were witnessing this stuffed teddy bear begin to move. We looked at Alec, but she wasn't touching the teddy bear. It wiggled all on its own. First its feet, then its little tummy, then its arms, then...

"Happy Birthday!"

"What? What was that?" I could not believe my ears, nor did Gloria by the way her eyes opened wide. Kayla stood back in awe. Again, we heard it.

"Happy Birthday!" The words came from Gloria's gift.

I felt as if Frosty the Snowman had popped out of the TV, but no, it was this little teddy bear in front of us saying those words. Now, our eyes were as wide open and non-blinking as this teddy bear's eyes.

"What is everyone looking at?" he inquired.

"Why, you, of course." Alec answered the bear. "Please forgive them, but they are new at this. You should have seen the one we call Don when he heard me talk for the first time."

The teddy bear took his paws, held his little belly and giggled. "I bet that was fun to watch, hey? By the way, my name is Teddy, as in teddy bear. Only it is spelled capital "T". Small "e". Small "d". Hyphen. Capital "D". Ted-D."

"Well, if that isn't unique." Kayla Kitten stated.

"Thank you." He took a bow, then asked, "Now, who would all of you be?"

After the shock factor wore off a bit and introductions were given, gift wrap was picked up and put away, the night found us with Alec curled up in Kayla Kitten's lap while Ted-D snuggled into Momma giving her big, little bear hugs every now and then. "I feel as if I am finally home," he cooed.

"You are, Ted-D. You are. We are a family. You, I, Alec, Kayla, and Don."

"Oh, that sounds so nice, Momma. So very, very nice. I believe I shall like it here."

"I believe you will, too," Alec stated. "These people are very nice. Strange at times, but nice."

"You really think you are funny, don't you?" Don asked of Alec.

"I do. I really, truly do." And then she laughed. We all laughed.

***

The days and months following Gloria's birthday were some of the most interesting I had ever lived. Now, don't get me wrong, there are plenty of times I get amazed at what I witness in my world. Like the birth of my first child, these times I shall always remember with great fondness, too. Not that you don't think fondly of the others that follow, but these "firsts" really make an impression.

I was becoming more accustomed to Alec-the-Cat being able to speak, and quite intelligently, too. Ted-D took me awhile to fathom, but he had already attached himself to my heart. Unlike Alec who had embedded her nails into my heart in love, Ted-D had gotten my heart with his cuteness, so to say.

With each rotation of the planet, our family, as "unique" as it was, seemed to feel more complete. Momma, Daddy, daughter Kayla Kitten, Alec-the-Cat, and Ted-D Bear. Not the family I had ever dreamed of gaining, but definitely full of the love I had always hoped would fill my home when I got older. A family I was so very fortunate in belonging.

Ted-D and Alec became very close with one another. Some mornings they would be the first to awaken and they would tiptoe into the living room to play or look out the window watch-ing the birds, cars, and people go by. For Gloria and me, we would wake up to the sound of laughter. A sound we cherished, not only in the knowledge that Alec and Ted-D loved one another so deeply, but we knew the weekend was upon us and we could spend the time together. No work away from home. Yay!

Sometimes we would lie in bed, listening to the two of them. Some days they would talk about what they were watching outside the Bay Window District, other days they would tell each other jokes. It was so gosh darn cute. Then Ted-D would get on Alec like she was a horse and ride her bareback into the bedroom, Alec jumping up on the bed, Ted-D hugging Alec's neck tightly, whilst yelling "Yee Ha, time to get up Momma, Daddy. Alec is hungry!"

Then Ted-D would jump off Alec and get on Momma's forehead, bend over, look her right in the eyes and say, "I love you, Momma." Looking over at me, he would finish with, "And Daddy, too." Then he would smile. Meanwhile, from beneath our chins, Alec would grab the blankets in her teeth and run backwards away from us, jumping off at the end of the bed. Our new alarm clocks. Got to love them.

The weekends never seemed to last long. The clock was always spinning at twice the speed of sound. Mondays finding Gloria and I, reluctantly, returning to the places which helped put food on the table and a roof over our heads.

Gloria's day began soon after the sun woke up, while mine began much later in the day, thankfully. Still, it was hard to leave Ted-D and Alec alone. No matter how much we knew they were good at not getting into trouble, we still feared something bad would happen at home; be it storms or other calamity.

We always tried to make sure they knew where to go in cases like this, so as we might be able to get them to safety as soon as we got to them. They listened well.

***

Packing my lunch for the night, I looked down at Alec and Ted-D who were playing on the kitchen floor.

"So, do you two have any big plans for the day?" I asked, closing the cooler I used as a lunch box.

"Not really, Daddy," Ted-D replied rolling the blue ball to Alec.

"Probably look out the back window today and watch the birds and bunnies," Alec said as she rolled the ball back to Ted-D.

"Alec's funny when she watches the birdies, Daddy."

"Now, why is that Ted-D?" I asked.

"She makes these little noises and then she sits up on her butt and paws at the window." Ted-D sat on his butt and mimicked pawing at an imaginary window. "It's funny."

"I can't help it, Ted-D. It's just something inside me from when my kind were hunters, and the world was full of big Pterodactyls."

"Ptero what?" Ted-D asked.

"Big dinosaur birds, Ted-D. We would hunt them in packs for our meals. MMMMMM, tasty."

"Really, Alec?"

"I think so, Ted-D." Alec laughed.

"Oh, Alec. You got me good." Ted-D giggled.

"Well, I am going to miss you two while I'm at work. But I'll be thinking of you."

"We will be thinking of you too, Daddy. Is Momma going to come home at the usual time tonight? I always get that mixed up."

Alec looked at Ted-D, then rolled over and scratched an ear, all while answering Ted-D's question. "She'll be a little late tonight, little brother. Remember she goes up by Great Uncle Wayne on these days."

"Oh, that's right. I think I may need a calendar to remember Momma's schedule. She is so busy I just can't remember all she does."

"No calendar needed. I will help you remember, Ted-D."

"Thank you, Alec. I don't know what I would have done with a calendar anyway. Maybe I could have colored it though." Ted-D smiled at his reply. "I do like coloring."

"Yes, you do." Alec agreed. "So very good at it, too."

"Well, I must get going to work now, my buddies. You two be good and I'll see you when I get home, OK?"

"OK, Daddy-O, we love you." Alec jumped up on the counter to give my face a lick. Ted-D was right behind her.

"Here's a big bear hug, Daddy. We'll miss you. Hurry home."

"I will. Love you both."

In unison, they both sang, "We love you, too." They are a pair.

Backing the truck out of the driveway, I noticed the two of them in the window. Alec and Ted-D both blowing me kisses. I blew some kisses back in return. Driving away I was happy they got along so well. I am sure they will have a good time. I just hope they remember to take their nap before Momma gets home.

The hours were put in at work for another day in history that no one will want to read about, so suffice it to say, I got home at the usual time and as I opened the door, I found both Ted-D and Alec waiting for me. Talk about feeling the love.

"Hi, Daddy. Did you miss us?" Ted-D whispered. "Momma's sleeping." Alec rubbed her body against my ankles as I looked down at Ted-D who looked up at me with those big brown eyes.

"Yes, I did," I whispered back.

"How much did you miss us?" Ted-D questioned.

"This much," I replied, opening my arms in a wide stretch, then scooping the both of them up and giving them a big hug. "Want a bigger hug? I can give you a bigger hug if you wish."

"No, Daddy, that is big enough," Alec answered, jumping out of my arms. "You do know I'm claustrophobic the way it is."

"Oh, but I can't help myself," I replied as I tickled Ted-D in my arms, Ted-D trying to cover his belly up and laughing. "I missed you two so much." I smiled. "Now," putting Ted-D down, "You said Momma was sleeping?"

"Yes, she went to bed early. She has another headache."

"That isn't good. Probably the change in the weather again."

Ted-D nodded, "That's what she said, too."

Alec bounced down the stairs, "Want to play, Daddy?" She asked. Then, without waiting for me to reply, she picked up a toy in her mouth and brought it upstairs to me.

"I see Momma bought you some new toys, ey, Alec?" I picked the mouse up to toss back down the stairs for her to gather again. "It feels so soft. Wow, they are making these so life-like" and then it moved. "What the heck?" I exclaimed, the mouse dropping out of my hand, wriggling in the floor by my feet. "I thought it was real."

"It is, Daddy. I thought you said there weren't any mice in the house. That's what Alec told me today." Ted-D's voice came from behind -and above- my shoulder. There, on top of the fridge, legs hanging over the freezer door, his rump dusty from ancestors prior, was Ted-D laughing.

"Well, you two got me good." I laughed. "OK, so, you found one," my voice sounding more depressed now. "I am happy you found him, but you know I try to make sure this house is taken care of, no holes in the foundation or anything. I don't know how he got in here. Thanks for finding him."

By this time, Alec had gone down the stairs and brought up a second mouse.

"Oh, you must be joking. At least it's only two. Still, impossible."

Alec didn't stay around to hear me say this as she had already gone down the stairs to retrieve a third mouse.

"How can this be? I hope that's all of them."

"Yes, that's all of them." Alec answered, spitting the mouse onto the floor by the other two.

"They must have come through the dryer vent." I said, my voice lacking optimism.

"I don't think so, Daddy," Ted-D replied from his perch. "We looked and there weren't any holes in the pipes. Or anywhere else."

"Unbelievable. Well," I looked at Alec sitting there in front of me, "it looks as if I'll be trying to locate their entrance tomorrow."

"I hope you find it," Alec licked her lips. "They are not very tasty. Yuck!"

"So, I take it that means you wish to be fed your usual tomorrow morning again?"

"Yes, it does. I'm sure you won't forget as I'll be waking you up. You know how this works."

"Yes, I do." I smiled at the two of them. "You two are a team, a good team. I'm glad you're here with us."

"Us, too. We love you, Daddy." Ted-D put a paw over one eye. "I'm pirate Ted-D." He laughed.

Putting a hand over one eye myself, I piped, "And pirates need their sleep. Let us get to bed now, OK? I love you guys."

Not to be left out, Alec joined in, "Argh. Right back at you, Daddy-O."

V
Co-author

I was glad to be home this weekend. Work sucked as it has been recently. I didn't mind my job, nor the people I worked with, but the management was almost non-existent. Because of that, we could not keep people, we were losing the ex- perienced ones, and the rest of us had to pick up the slack.

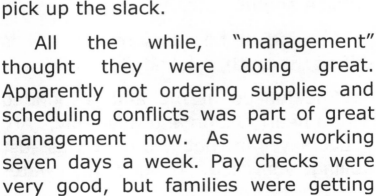

All the while, "management" thought they were doing great. Apparently not ordering supplies and scheduling conflicts was part of great management now. As was working seven days a week. Pay checks were very good, but families were getting stressed, and children didn't know their parents as they once had.

Oh well, no need to fret about that today. Today was going to be an in-the-home-office-day, complete with a perking pot of go-go juice and putting words into a story. Hopefully this book sells.

Tossing the blankets off, I eased my legs over the edge of the bed when I heard something, or rather, someone. It was Alec.

As to not wake Gloria, I bent down closer to Alec and asked, "what's up buddy?"

Alec replied with, "I need to go outside and go potty."

Looking at her, unsure if she was telling the truth, I asked, "Really?"

She looked at me and responded with a hearty laugh and this reply, "Are you crazy? I'm not a dog, I was just pulling your leg. I need my water changed. It's dirty." I couldn't help but laugh.

"You're joking, right? I mean, I've seen you lick your own butt and you are worried that your water is dirty?"

"How do you think I clean my tongue after I lick my butt? Toilet water?" She looked at me like I was crazy. "Again, I am not a dog."

I would find many of my days to begin like that here forward. But I was OK with that. Alec had an attitude, that was for sure, but I enjoyed her wit. Thankfully.

Sitting in the office, fireplace flickering non-burning flames, ceiling fan on - as were my slippers and bathrobe - I listened to the pot of coffee perking from the kitchen. This was my little bit of heaven. With that I cracked the window open ever so slightly to get some fresh air. Behind me, I heard footsteps.

"Good morning, Honey," Gloria barely got the words out of her mouth before a yawn came rushing out of her.

"Good morning, Love. Did you sleep well?" I looked at Alec rubbing up against Gloria's ankle.

"Yes, not too bad. I wish I could have slept longer but ---" she looked down at Alec.

"Hey, I'm hungry. You do know these paws of mine can't open food cans, don't cha? Open a few cans and let them out for me and you'll get to sleep in. Until then, well, feed me. Please." Alec purred as she wrapped her tail around Gloria's leg.

"I hear you. Guess I won't be sleeping in anytime soon as I am not going to leave food open for you."

"Suit yourself. Suit yourself." Alec smiled.

Gloria blew me a kiss and turned towards the kitchen. "Writing day today?"

"Yup. If you don't mind, that is."

"Not at all. It will be nice to stay home and relax for once. We've been going a lot lately."

"Yes. If it is not one thing, it is another. Otherwise, it is a project of one sort or another. Today, though, is writing day."

"Sounds great." And with that, Gloria went into the kitchen to feed Alec, who, by that time was already in the kitchen waiting to dine. I turned back toward the window, watching the birds eat while listening to the perk-perk-perk of the coffee pot in the distance.

"Did you fall asleep?" It was Gloria behind me.

I opened my eyes, turned my chair from the window to face Gloria and said, "Well, no. I was simply thinking about how I was going to go about writing today." She laughed.

"Here, I'll help you." She walked to where I was sitting and took my hands in hers. "You put your fingers on this here keyboard and you begin typing. Whatever comes into your head, you type. When you finish the book, then I edit. See? Simple, isn't it?"

I smiled. "You would think so."

"Now here's a cup of coffee for you. Get to writing now." She handed me the cup of go-go juice and laughed. "It is almost like talking, only you need to type your words."

"I know, Love. I know. Thank you."

"You're welcome. Now, get to work. I'll close the door so it's quiet for you." With that, coffee in hand, I let the words in my head take control.

With a few more pages written and an empty cup, I proceeded to the kitchen for a refill of go-go juice. Gloria was finishing the drying of last nights dishes that she had just washed when I entered.

"Boo!" I yelled at her back.

"Boo back at you," was her reply.

"I can't understand how I never get you to jump."

"You have to remember, Honey, Kayla did that stuff to me a lot when she was growing up. I guess you could say I've become immune to "Boo!"" She laughed.

"Yes, well, have you become immune to this?" I asked as I put the coffee cup down on the counter and whisked her into my arms. I began to lead her into a slow dance to whatever that song was that she was listening to on her phone.

"It has been a long time since we've danced." She put her head into the crook of my neck and sighed.

"Always busy, we are, my Love." I put my head against hers.

Together, for the three minutes or so the song lasted, we melded into one another, two spirits as one. It was total bliss for the two of us.

When the song ended, we heard laughter coming from the living room doorway to the kitchen. Turning to face that direction, we saw Alec and Ted-D, laughing, Alec holding Ted-D in her arms, the two of them having a grand time dancing themselves.

"I must say, you two, you are doing a very fine job dancing."

"Thank you, Daddy." Ted-D replied. "We tried to dance like you and Momma."

"Looks like you two are professionals," Momma chimed in. "Is Daddy a good teacher, Alec?"

"Yes, he is," Alec replied with a smile.

I looked at Alec, then at Gloria. "Well, Alec and I talk together, too." I smiled.

In the kitchen that morning a forever moment to remember was made.

***

"MMph!"

I turned from the keyboard towards the closed door only to see Alec attempting to get through the cat door into the office.

"Stuck there, buddy?" I laughed. "Maybe you should cut back on your eating."

"Not funny, word man. You could have splurged on the cat door instead of the hamster door."

"You do realize that is a cat door. I bought the biggest one they had."

"I don't know what is wrong with you two-legged creatures. You think you're so smart. Yet, when it comes to getting a cat door you get me a door for a mouse."

"I thought you said it was a hamster door?"

"You know what I mean." Alec growled at me as she pulled in her hind quarters.

"Now, now. I told you that was the largest cat door they offered."

Alec sat herself by my feet, looked up and stated, "You do realize I am related to the King of the Jungle."

"Doesn't mean you are the King of the Jungle, not even close in size there, buddy."

Jumping up on her window seat, glaring at me, she asked, "What are you trying to do there, write the next big novel? Perhaps "The Shining" or is it more or less going to be titled, "Fire Starter for Your Next Campfire?"" Alec rolled onto her back, legs in the air, laughing.

"I almost agree with you there, buddy. And that hurts. The reviews I have received in the past for my other books, well, for the majority, the people LIKE what I write about and how I write. Still, I believe it is my marketing that sucks. It's not easy being a self-published writer."

Turning around to face me, she asked, "You are going to quit writing then?"

"No, why would I do that?"

"If you are spending your money on marketing these books you say people LIKE to read but they aren't buying them, then, why do it?"

"Because I enjoy it. And, you never know. Maybe I will get a movie contract or at least a major selling book out there. Stephen King didn't do it over night."

"Well, you aren't either." Alec sat up and licked her butt. Flicking her tongue, she continued. "Maybe you need some extra help there, Stephanie Queen."

"Huh? Stepha---"

"It's a play upon Stephen King. You sure are slow in the mornings, aren't you?"

I had to agree with her, I was slow in the mornings. Never did like the rising sun except when I was younger and had partied until dawn. Heck, back then I would go from the party to my day job. Never believed in missing work.

While Alec soaked up the sun like a tuxedoed sponge on steroids, I plucked away on the keyboard for the next five hours. Neither of us left our perches except to refill my coffee cup and Alec to ... nope, she didn't leave her spot at all.

"So, what 'cha writing there today?" Alec asked, then yawned like the King of the Jungle she thought she was.

"It's another book consisting of short stories taken from my life experiences. Readers seemed to have really enjoyed the first book."

"Is that so? What is it called? How to die by the pen?"

"Oh great, you're waking up." Alec purred and smiled all at the same time. "No, it is called "We Really Need To Laugh", written under my pen name of Alec Gould. It's how we should enjoy life no matter how bad it gets. To find the fun stuff and happy moments when we can in order to get through the hard times when they happen. It reminds us that life is too short to be worrying all the time. We should enjoy."

"Well, it does sound like a book that would fulfill some people's voids. Maybe I'll read your first book later."

"You can read?" I asked, turning towards her.

"Why, of course I can read. All cats can read." She looked at me like she was surprised at my not knowing this. "We have nine lives, you know. What do you think we do, sleep all the time? We pride ourselves in our high IQs."

"I must admit, you do sound educated, for a cat. By the way, what number are you on?"

"What do you mean, what number am I on?"

"You know, what number life. 1, 2, 3 or higher?"

"First off, we never discuss that. Second, we never dwell on that. Third, and this you should know, one should never waste their lives dwelling on matters they cannot do anything about. What number life am I on? It does not matter to you, nor to me. It only matters that we enjoy life as we do. With one another, with love."

"You are very profound this morning."

"I like to be profound every now and then. But I would rather hack up a hair ball and watch you clean it up. It is much more fun than being profound all the time." And with that, Alec proceeded to Ted-D's room.

"Hey, Ted-D, would you like me to read you a funny book?"

I didn't say a word, I just knew. Smart aleck cat. I had to chuckle. She is such a good girl and she and Ted-D get along so well. It melts my heart. More than that, I can't believe how much she is growing on me.

Later that evening, after another hour of writing, Alec came into my office.

"I didn't want to say anything while you and Momma were dining tonight, but I read your book today."

"And?" I inquired.

"And, if you don't mind, I thought I would offer my editing services. Free of charge, of course."

"Editing services? Free of charge?"

"You heard me correctly. I found your book rather appealing, but in all regards, it lacked in certain areas. Areas in which I believe I may be of some assistance."

"Is that so? How could you possibly help me write better than I do. You are a cat."

"You are correct, Daddy-O, that I am. Yet, there is more to me than what the eye sees. Give me an opportunity to prove my worth. That is, if you do not mind."

"It couldn't hurt, right."

"Right. Then, you don't mind?"

"No, not at all. But" I added, "we will need to get a spritzer."

"A spritzer? What the heck is a spritzer?" asked Alec.

"Well, I'm not sure if that is the correct word for this item, but what I am thinking about is a thing I used on my daughters when they were babies. I used it to clear out their nose when they were sick. A nasal aspirator boogie bulb."

"A nasal aspirator boogie bulb?"

"Yes. A nasal aspirator boogie bulb."

Alec looked at me like I had lost it. "Now, why would you want to clean out my nose? First, I am not sick. Second, I'm a cat, I can clean out my own nose. I am not a baby."

"You didn't let me finish, buddy. I would use this spritzer like a baster, squeezing the bulb to push air out and that would remove whatever hair you lose onto the computer monitor."

Alec gave me a quizzical look as I continued.

"With a spritzer, I would not need to use my fingers to remove your hair and thus, no fingerprints would be left upon the monitor's screen."

"OK, that makes sense. But are you sure it's not your hair that is being lost?

Oh wait, your hair is grey, mine is black. OK, nasal aspirator boogie bulb it is."

And with that, the next few years brought us a new chapter.

VI
Big Sister Alec

It had been a sad year for all of us. Not the whole year, but after the accident this past spring, it took a hit upon us. Stress and heartache seemed to be one of those visitors who didn't want to leave.

Ted-D had been very close to his grandparents and when they both died in a car accident, Ted-D was unsure how to act. We were all unsure how to act.

Being that Ted-D's grandparents were Gloria's parents; they both could hear Alec-the-Cat talk. That also meant, they could understand Ted-D. The three of them were very close.

Unbeknownst to the other people who had shown up for the funeral, Ted-D whimpered and Gloria and I tried to console him the best we could. It is not good for Ted-D to get wet anyway, but when it is his own tears, it hurts that much more. It broke our hearts to see Ted-D so sad.

We managed to get on with our lives the best we could, but you could feel the void that Gloria's parents had left behind. They were special people to us both and especially Ted-D, who had no other two-legged companion that understood him. It was Gloria, Kayla, me, and Alec now. We were happy to have one another. Ted-D was truly loved.

Even though death takes a lot out of everyone, birthdays are a day to celebrate. Even when one is sad, we must remember the happy times to keep enjoyment in our lives. With that, we woke up to Ted-D's birthday.

Not one for getting up early, I must say it was a beautiful morning. As the sun cleared the darkness for me to see my slippers, the birds sang their morning tunes outside our bedroom window.

Gloria was snoring so I knew she was in a deep sleep; Alec was curled up by her feet and Ted-D was cuddled in Momma's arms. To the tune of a perking pot of coffee and a pop of the toaster, I slowly began to wake up.

Going outside with a cup of go-go juice, I watched the black cap chickadees arrive at the feeders to get that one special seed. Never more than one at a time. Not like some of the other birds that came in for their feedings. Nope. The chickadees always came in for one seed then took off to eat it elsewhere. They would then return for another. Unlike the other birds who would shake their beaks through the seeds, looking for a few of their prime choice seeds while sending many to the ground for the chipmunks and bunnies.

With my cup emptied, I decided to take a walk through the back wildflower garden. I was looking for butterflies shedding the morning dew from their beings, the slight breeze or sun helping them do so. They could then take off in flight for the day. It always brought back memories when I took nature photos. Yup. Best time of day for butterfly and dragonfly photos as they couldn't leave their perch until their wings had dried. Almost like a plane with ice on its wings, they couldn't fly with the dew on theirs. No luck today, maybe tomorrow I'll see some.

Back at the door, I took one last gulp of the fresh air and headed back to the kitchen for a refill of caffeine. Gloria was now up, as was Alec and Ted-D. Momma and Ted-D were at the counter getting Alec her breakfast when I walked into the room.

"Good morning, everyone. Did all have a good night of sleep?" I bent down to pet Alec and plant a kiss upon Ted-D's head, finishing up with a special smooch for Gloria, which landed upon her cheek when she turned her face from me.

"Good morning, Honey. Sorry, I just got up and haven't had a chance to brush my teeth yet." She looked down at Alec-the-Cat.

Alec looked up at me, "First things first, Daddy-O. I need to eat."

Looking down at Alec I replied, "One wouldn't know that if you hadn't told me."

"You do realize I know where you sleep, right? Well, keep talking like that and I'll be sleeping on your pillow tonight."

"Oh sure, you can joke with me, but I can't with you."

"Not when it comes to my weight, you can't. I don't joke about your lack of hair on that chrome dome of yours now, do I?"

"Point well taken, my friend. Point well taken." I smiled at Alec. "Enjoy your breakfast." Turning towards Ted-D I asked, "So, I hear it's a special day for someone in this room, am I correct?"

With eyes wide open Ted-D stated, "Yes, it's my birthday."

"So, it is. How would you like all of us to take a ride to the park today, like we always do?"

Ted-D looked away, but we could see he had tears in his eyes. Alec took her tail and wiped them away before they soaked into Ted-D's coat. "Ted-D, why don't you join me for breakfast?"

"OK," then Ted-D rode on Alec's back to Alec's dinner nook.

I looked over at Gloria who also had a tear on her cheek. I removed it with a caress from my finger.

"I know, Love. But I think we should keep their memory alive. You know your parents always enjoyed a day in the park for Ted-D's birthday. We shouldn't forget those times."

"I understand." She sighed. "We shouldn't forget those times. Still. This is the first time without my parents being with us to share in Ted-D's birthday."

"I know, Love. I know. It is going to be difficult for all of us." I put my arms around her.

* * *

Finished with buckling Ted-D into his car seat and Momma comfortable in the passenger seat, Alec watched out the kitchen window. I proceeded to get behind the steering wheel.

"Are we all ready, troops?" I called out.

"Yes, Daddy. All ready," Ted-D replied from the back seat.

"All ready, Honey," Gloria smiled.

"OK then. Here we go." And with that I put the car into gear. Gloria and Ted-D waved to Alec, watching as she got smaller in the distance.

Ted-D yelled out the window, "We'll see you in a few hours Alec." Alec yawned in reply and waved her paw.

All things considered; it was a beautiful day for a drive. Blue sky, not a cloud to be seen, well no rain clouds at least. A few cumulus clouds, that was all. White and puffy against the blue, they looked like cotton floating on the bluest of seas.

To keep Ted-D from worrying about being in the park absent of his grandparents, Gloria played "spotting" games with him. Do you spot a yellow car or a mailbox? Games like that. Me? I had my mind busy with driving safely, but I was also looking for those items.

The day was not going to be easy on any of us, but with hope, it would be a good birthday day for Ted-D.

Although Ted-D didn't eat foods, he still enjoyed people watching so we stopped in at his favorite place to do so. Gloria and I had our pizza slices and soda, Ted-D had new people to watch and learn things from.

"Did you notice that man over there, Daddy? How he uses a cane to help him walk? And the other man with him also has a cane. They must be friends, hey Daddy?"

"You may be right there, Ted-D", I acknowledged as I stole a glance at the men Ted-D was talking about. "You are observant, my boy." I smiled proudly at him. He seemed to be growing up so fast, even if he were a little teddy bear.

"I like to watch and learn, Daddy. The world is so big. Especially when one is as little as me and Alec. It seems so much bigger and there is always so much going on."

"You are correct on that. So much going on. And learning about what goes on around you is important as it helps you learn bigger things then. Like building blocks. Learn little things and then you get to learn bigger things."

"I wish Alec could have come along with us though, Daddy. That would have been more fun. I like it when she is with me."

"I know it would have been more fun with her by your side, but you know she doesn't like to take rides. She prefers to stay home and then she looks forward to you sharing all that you had seen and done."

"That is true. She does like that. Just as I like it when she shares with me what happens out the window when I am away. We take good care of each other, don't we, Daddy?"

"Yes, you do. Your Momma and I are so glad you two do that for each other." I smiled at Gloria.

"It is nice to have a friend like Alec, isn't it Ted-D? One you can share ideas and do stuff with." Momma smiled.

"Not only is Alec my friend, but she is also my big sister. I love her so very, very much."

"I can see that she also loves you very, very much, Ted-D." Momma said. "You two are a special pair of friends. Big sister and little brother."

Ted-D pulled his legs to his chest and giggled. "That we are, Momma. That we are."

With dinner done and back out on the road, we didn't have far to travel now. While Gloria held my hand, Ted-D stared more intently out the window. The sky was still blue and the clouds a puffy white. I believed it was still going to be a good day. Rough, but good.

Thirty minutes later found us pulling into the parking stall at the park. This was no ordinary park either. It was the park where I had played as a youngster.

The playground had changed, the equipment having been upgraded and all, but my memories were as vivid as if I were the one that was going to be playing on the toys today.

As I put the car into park I called out, "We're here Ted-D." Ted-D was silent. He stared out the window, not moving a muscle.

"It will be OK, dear," Gloria said. "I am sure Grandma and Grandpa are happy that you are here today to celebrate your birthday."

"Do you think they are?"

"Yes, I truly do believe that. They always liked it when their Ted-D enjoyed playing here with them. Remember how they would be beaming those big smiles?"

"Yes, I do," Ted-D began to smile a bit himself. "They had nice smiles, didn't they, Momma?"

"Yes, they did," Gloria replied, hiding her tears behind the pillow she used for her neck on long drives. "I suppose we better get out and enjoy this great weather, huh?" And with that, we all held hands and paws, skipping our way to the playground area.

"So, where would you like to play first?"

"On the swings. That's where Grandpa and I would go first. Can you push me, Daddy?"

"I sure can Ted-D. Under-ducks too?"

"Yes, Daddy. Like Grandpa used to give me."

As Ted-D was being pushed ever so slowly he could feel Grandpa's hands on his back. Yet, when Daddy gave Ted-D an under-duck Daddy would be the one coming from under Ted-D, not Grandpa.

Next Ted-D wanted to go to the slide. And just like Grandma, Momma waited for Ted-D to come down the slide to meet her at the bottom. Just like he always remembered at every birthday. Ted-D, Momma, Daddy, Grandma, and Grandpa playing in the park.

Still, it was not the same. But something told him it would be alright. Ted-D took a break on top of the Lady Bug.

As he sat on the lady bug's head, Ted-D saw a pair of pelicans flying above. Ted-D stared and pointed.

Momma and Daddy looked up. "Those are pelicans, aren't they, Ted-D?" Daddy asked.

For the first time on Ted-D's birthday, a big smile came across his face. "Grandpa always liked pelicans and Grandma always liked lady bugs. It's almost like they are watching us play."

"I think you are right, Ted-D." Momma smiled. "They will always be with you."

"And you too, Momma?" Ted-D asked.

"Yes, and with Daddy and Mamma." Ted-D saw a tear in his parent's eyes. "You miss Grandma and Grandpa, too?"

"Yes, we do. Death is always hard to handle, no matter how old a person gets. But we know they will always be watching over us."

Daddy wiped a tear away and smiled. "Momma's correct, Ted-D. Death is hard on everyone. Yet, we keep the memories alive by talking about them and thinking about them, too."

"You mean like we are doing today? Celebrating my birthday like we always did with Grandma and Grandpa? A...a tradition?"

"Yes, Ted-D, a tradition. To keep their memory alive. To remember fondly the times that we've shared."

"That's nice, Daddy. I like this tradition."

As Ted-D slid off the ladybug and ran towards the merry-go-round, Momma smiled at Daddy. Ted-D yelled over his shoulder, "Daddy, can you push while Momma holds onto me?"

"I sure can, Ted-D," Daddy said.

Ted-D had already climbed aboard the merry-go-round as Momma and Daddy reached him. Momma sat down facing outward as Ted-D sat next to her, her arms around Ted-D so he wouldn't fall off. Daddy began pushing the merry-go-round.

"Faster Daddy. Faster," yelled Ted-D. Momma smiled while Daddy listened to Ted-D's directions. As Daddy pushed the merry-go-round a little bit faster, Ted-D thought he had seen Grandma and Grandpa standing nearby smiling and waving at Ted-D. Ted-D smiled and let out a "Weeeeeee".

As the merry-go-round slowed to a halt, Daddy asked Ted-D if it would be OK to visit where Grandma and Grandpa were buried. Ted-D was hesitant but agreed. "Yes, Daddy, I still need to be near them on my birthday."

The drive to the cemetery was filled with tears as Ted-D began to once again know he would never have Grandma and Grandpa hold him in their arms, but he knew everything was going to be OK. He didn't know how, but somehow, he knew.

Daddy pulled into the drive and parked the car. Momma got Ted-D and held him in her arms. Ted-D looked around and asked, "What is this place called again, Momma?"

"This is called a cemetery, Ted-D. It is where we bury our loved ones so we can come and visit whenever we wish."

Wide-eyed, Ted-D hugged Momma closer to him. "There is nothing to be afraid of, Ted-D. Listen. Hear the birds singing. They are saying all is good."

As Momma held onto Ted-D, they followed Daddy to where Grandma and Grandpa were buried. Ted-D got down and stood in front of the headstone. He was very quiet.

"Did you want to say a few words to them, Ted-D? Maybe tell them how you played in the park today for your birthday?"

"I can do that, Momma? Will they hear me?"

"Yes," Momma replied.

"Will they talk to me too?" Ted-D asked in awe.

"It may take a while for you to hear, but yes, they will talk with you. You'll be able to hear them in your heart and in your mind. Would you like Daddy and me to leave you alone so you can have some time with Grandma and Grandpa?"

"Uh. OK. I think. Will I be OK alone here?"

"You'll be OK, Ted-D. We won't be far," Daddy stated.

"OK," and with that, Ted-D knelt by the headstone. Momma and Daddy went for a walk, not too far away, but far enough that Ted-D could be alone with his grandparents.

Sometime later Ted-D stood up and called to his parents, "You can come back now. I'm OK."

When they got near Ted-D, he had a surprise for them. He had put some kitty knick-knacks near the headstone. "Alec doesn't like to go for rides, but I didn't want Grandma and Grandpa to forget about Alec."

"That is so kind of you, Ted-D. Are you sure you wish to leave them here though? I know you carry them around like lucky charms."

"Yes, Momma, I want to leave them here. We can always come back and visit them with Grandma and Grandpa."

"Well, Ted-D, you are growing up so big. OK then. Would you like to get your picture taken with Grandma and Grandpa?"

Ted-D looked shocked! Momma explained, "I mean, would you like to sit next to the headstone and have your picture taken?"

Ted-D smiled as he skipped to the headstone. "Can I give them a hug, too?"

Momma and Daddy nodded yes and Ted-D hugged Grandma's corner by her name, then he hugged Grandpa's corner by his name. "Did you get the photos? All of them?" Ted-D asked with a big smile.

"Yes, we did. All of them." Momma and Daddy had big smiles, too.

As they drove out of the cemetery Ted-D yelled out the window and waved. "I will be back to visit again." And then Ted-D fell asleep.

When they got home, Ted-D ran into the bedroom by Alec and woke her up. "Was it a good Happy Birthday Day, Ted-D?"

"Yes. It was. It started out as a sad Happy Birthday Day. But then I saw Grandma and Grandpa in a lot of places.

I saw Grandpa in the pelicans, Grandma in the ladybug and you know what?" Ted-D beamed and before Alec could ask "What?" Ted-D shared, "They both sang Happy Birthday to me!"

"They did?" Alec asked. "How so?"

"They sang it in my memory. I heard them in my mind, and I felt them in my heart, too."

"They will always be with us, won't they, Ted-D?" asked Alec.

"Yes, they will" and Ted-D fell asleep within Alec's tail. Alec purred. Alec was happy for Ted-D on this happy, sad Birthday Day. Alec knew Ted-D would be OK.

VII
Simple Things

Winter, although just beginning, was taking its toll upon my body. I didn't look forward to shoveling the white crystals of winter anymore. Sure, they were nice  to look at as they gently came down from the heavens but when it came time to remove them from the drive or the sidewalks, my back went out on strike.

"Honey, you do realize you are not as young as you once were. None of us are." Ted-D and Alec watched their mom and dad talking in the kitchen, giggling to themselves at what Momma had just said to Daddy.

"I heard that," Daddy looked at Ted-D and Alec. "You also heard your Momma state that we are all getting older. That included you two."

"Doesn't matter, Daddy. It's still funny." Alec replied as she and Ted-D rolled on the carpet with laughter. Daddy smiled at them.

Gloria continued. "We can afford it now. Why not get one of those nice garden tractors with a snowblower on it. You'd probably find it more enjoyable. Out there in your coonskin hat and skunk mittens. A regular old Red Green." Gloria smiled at her wit.

"Do you really think I should buy one of those? They aren't cheap."

"Neither is you missing work due to your back issues. What happens if your back goes out and you can't work anymore? Then what?"

"Then I get to retire?"

"Not funny, Honey. Why don't you research those machines and get yourself a real nice one? Get a lawn roller with it too so we can get this lawn back to nice and flat. I hate the thought about stumbling on those rare occasions when I do go outside."

"OK, Love. If you really don't mind, I'll do that. Always thought it would be nice to have one of those but never thought it possible for us."

I poured myself a fresh cup of go-go juice from the percolator and retreated to the office. I thought to myself, "This should be fun. I never thought about looking at these machines today, or ever. Dreams do become reality when you work every day towards your goals together."

As I sat in my office chair, elbows upon the table I used as a desk, hands clasped and face resting within, I happened to notice a "scent". It reminded me of when I was a youngin' playing out in the woods and my brother and I came upon a dead animal. Not much left of it, bones mainly. It seemed as if it used to be an opossum, but we were not sure. At least the jawbone with its teeth looked like it had been like that in life. Still, the reason for that memory coming back to me at this instant is the aroma that surrounded that death area. It smelled like bone marrow wisping in the air and that is what I had just smelled upon my hands. Maybe I was closer to death than I realized? Thankfully, Alec wandered in to save my insane thoughts for another day.

"So, you checking out those pricey machines there, Daddy-O?" She jumped up on her window perch and looked me in the eyes.

"Yes, why not? It is something I had thought would be nice to add to the arsenal of lawn equipment I have. This would really make things easier, although I do not see myself using the mower. Not with the lawn size we have. Still, maybe, down the line I may."

"One never knows what the future holds, does it old man?"

"No. We don't," I replied, ignoring the old man part. "Now, I better start checking these machines over and see what fits our budget and our needs."

"OK. I think I'll just lie here in the sun and lick my butt. I hope you don't mind."

"No, not at all, buddy. Lick away." I sniffed the air but no smell like before when I came into the room. That was good. Maybe Alec had gas and ran out then returned. She does have a warped sense of humor.

Sometime later, Gloria entered the office to find Alec purring on my lap, me rubbing her belly. "I thought you were going to look for that new toy of yours?"

"New toy?" Alec asked, her ears at full attention.

"I was talking to your daddy, Alec." Gloria laughed as Alec jumped down and walked past her in a huff, swishing her tail in the air.

"I did, but then Alec needed some attention."

Gloria smiled. "You two have become rather close, haven't you?"

"She's a good girl. Couldn't imagine life without her, that's for sure."

"Well, did you find anything that you liked?" Gloria inquired as she wrapped an arm around my shoulder, giving me a kiss on my thinning area.

"Yes, I did. But it cost a mint."

"So, what are you going to do? Shovel and then not be able to walk anymore. You must admit, after that last time, you got lucky. Even the doctor said he was surprised your back allows you to move as you do today. But one more time could put you down for good. You heard him yourself."

"I know, Love, I know."

"So, what did you find to park in that garden shed you call a barn?"

***

Two weeks later found me not only snow blowing the white stuff from our drive and sidewalk but also a few of our fellow neighbors. Yes, they liked my new toy, too.

Finished with clearing the snow, I entered the warmth of our home. For once in my life, a smile frozen upon my face from enjoying this weather. Tossing my coonskin hat and skunk gloves on the floor to dry by the side closet, Alec came running into the hallway, finishing with a giant leap into the furriness.

"Purr. Purrrrrrr."

"Is my buddy happy?"

"Purrrrr-fectly happy. This is the bestest. You saw me watching from the window, waiting for you to finish out there. I know you did." She smiled. "I enjoy these things too, you know? Oh, so soft, so very, very soft. Purrrrrr."

I left Alec to enjoy the furriness, put my slippers on and entered the kitchen. Spying Ted-D with his stuffed little mousie toy, Baby-M, I walked over to see how he was doing.

"Hi, Daddy. All done outside?"

"Yes, I am. Unless we get more snow, that should be it for today." I picked Ted-D up and gave him a great big teddy bear hug.

"Oh, Daddy. I love you, too."

"So, what are you up to today?"

"Not too much. Baby-M and I are just going to hang out together. Probably just watch people out the window. You know, some of them are crazy drivers. They don't even stop at the stop sign."

"I know. It's sad that they drive like that. I only hope no one gets hurt because of their actions."

"Honey, what are you doing today?" Gloria called from the bedroom.

I looked in to see her making the bed. "Not too much. Alec and I were just going to write some more in that new book. Why?"

"Well, I was hoping we could stay home today. No running around. Maybe you could grill out later, if you wish, or I could call for delivery?"

"No, staying home and grilling out sounds like a great idea. We have been so darn busy, again. We don't even know what it's like to be home much."

"I know. We are busy with other people's needs, moving, and so on, which takes a lot out of us. We don't move like we used to."

"No, we don't. Now, let me guess. I should get some brats out to defrost."

"If you don't mind. Thanks, Honey."

Replying in a hushed voice, "You're welcome, Love. Now. Do you mind if I do something a bit crazy?"

"Oh, no. I'm afraid to ask."

"You see Alec over there, rolling around in my hat and gloves, right?" Gloria nodded. "Well, I had seen a sheepskin rug for toddlers I had thought she may like. After seeing her now, if you don't mind, how about I order that for her? She could roll around on it anytime she wished, not just when I am out in the cold with that hat and those gloves."

"Oh, she would like that. Yes. That's a great idea."

"I'll make sure I order that after I grill out tonight."

"I appreciate you doing all that, Honey."

"You're welcome, Love. Maybe I'll have a campfire later, too. It has been ready since last fall."

"I know," Gloria stated. "See. We've been too busy."

I agreed, then took Ted-D and Baby-M to visit their friends of the Bay Window District to people watch. Relinquishing myself to the office, I remembered I had brats to take out of the freezer for tonight.

***

Alec slowly walked into the office and barely managed to get up on her windowsill platform. Leaving out a sigh she smiled at me as I typed what I thought might be the end of the new book. No one knew yet, where the end might be though.

"You enjoy your time with my hat and mittens there, my friend?" I asked, reaching out to pet her.

"Yes, immensely." Alec laid down to enjoy my tickling of her ears. "Those two items are like candy to my being. So soft, so, I don't know, so, I guess, almost like having my momma back with me. I can lick them mittens like I used to do with my momma and my siblings. Ah, memories." She rolled over to her side so I could give her that belly rub she liked so much.

"Yes, memories are nice to have. The happy ones, that is."

"Well, we can't forget the sad ones either, Daddy. The sad are just as important as the happy. All memories make us who we are at this very moment."

"You are the wise one, aren't you, Alec?"

"You don't get through life without learning. Even if you aren't trying to learn, one always picks up on stuff."

"Funny you say that." I picked her up and held her in my lap all while continuing to give her belly a rub. "I noticed how you had a wee bit of an issue jumping up on your perch there."

"What are you getting at?" Alec purred. "The sun was in my eyes."

Ignoring her comment, I went on talking, "As we all know, we are not getting any younger. I was wondering, how would you like me to get you some stairs to help you get up, like, say, on the bed and your window perch?"

"You would do that for me, Daddy?"

"Why, of course I would. You're my buddy. You mean the world to me. Not only that, but to Momma and Ted-D. And to Kayla Kitten, too. We all love you and want you to be able to enjoy life and have fun. Just like we all do."

"Wow. That is so nice of you. I was not expecting anything. Only belly rubs. And food. Definitely food. Thank you."

"No problem, buddy. I'll start looking right now for those stairs."

Alec turned over onto her belly and looked at the computer monitor. "Since they are for me," Alec purred, "I think I should be involved in the decision-making process, mmm, don't cha think, Daddy?"

"You are quite right there, my friend. Let me know when you see something you like."

An hour later and lighter in the wallet, Alec had chosen a set of stairs for getting on the bed and another set for getting up by the window. She even chose some nice bowls for her food and water.

"Nice choices there, Alec. I believe you will be spoiled when these items arrive. But you deserve all that we've ordered. Being such a great buddy and a big brother to Ted-D, too."

"I'm glad you didn't mind me asking about the bowls. It's just that I seem to have issues every now and then with swallowing. Perhaps, I just need to diet a bit?"

"We all could use some dieting, but I don't see any of us doing so. Especially with the Christmas season coming up." I rubbed her ear and continued, "We all enjoy our foods. And I believe it would not be easy for you to give up that potato chip time with Momma, would it?"

Alec laughed. "I do like my chip at night. And it is only one. Not like I eat it either, I just lick off the salt. MMMMM MMM."

"Well, did you want to work on the new book some more?"

"I've been thinking about that, Daddy and," Alec took a pause then sat up. "You have been doing so well writing this book, well, I'm thinking about allowing you to finish this book all by yourself. What do you think about that?"

"You would "allow" me to do that?" I said with a smirk and bunny ears.

"Yes, I would. I have complete confidence in your ability now to tell a story that the world would be in awe of, in a good way, of course, to read and tell others about." Alec licked her paw and, nonchalantly, rubbed it around her ear.

"Do you really think so?" I asked, staring her down to see if she was going to break out in laughter.

"Yes, I really think so. You have listened well and have done far better than I had expected. I am very proud of you, Daddy."

"Well, I guess I should say thank you. But ---," now this was where I took a pause in my words. "But I thought we were writing this book together."

"We still are. Only now, I guess you could say, I am going to be watching from a distance. Sort of like a ghost writer. Yes, I like that. Like a ghost writer. You will do well. You know the words; all you need to do is put them down in writing." Alec jumped on my lap and looked intently into my eyes. "You've got this. And...and I love you." She licked my chin.

"You're my buddy, Alec. And I love you." I gave her a kiss on her head. And with that I got a blanket for my lap and the two of us watched the snow erase this past year.

VIII
Sunset

The winter months, although a bit more enjoyable for Alec since her sheepskin rug dubbed Billie had arrived, the winter months thankfully passed by quickly. Quickly though, to find the heat of summer lurking like a match against the striker. This was springtime in Wisconsin.

Gloria and I had just gotten home from flying our drone, something we did not get a lot of time to do. I would commander the controls and Gloria would look through the goggles, enjoying the views.

"Mind if I turn the air conditioning on, Alec?"

"If you wish. Me? I'm a bit chilled, but I can curl up in this great box I got for Christmas."

"The one Kayla Kitten joked about with you?"

"That's the one. She thought it was a joke. Me? I thought I got a great gift. And it is."

"Yes. You really do enjoy that box. I'm happy for you, Alec."

Alec and I were in the office still writing that new book. The leaves had finally covered the branches and gave great homes to this year's birds.

"You're sounding a bit hoarse there, Alec. You get a cold?"

"You know I don't get sick," she glared at me. "I'm a healthy cat."

"Now, now. We all get sick at times."

Alec agreed, reluctantly. "I just don't care for being ill. It takes the fun out of everything."

Ted-D came around the corner. "What's the matter, big sister? Are you not feeling well?" Ted-D laid near Alec, pressing his head into Alec's belly. "You gurgled." Ted-D laughed.

Alec joined his sister in the laugh. "Yes, I seem to be doing more of that lately."

"You sound like a grizzly bear. Are you OK, Alec?" Ted-D looked up from his cuddle area.

"Just not feeling that well. There is a lot of stuff going 'round. Allergies, colds, and then that darn Covid." Alec put a paw around Ted-D. "Now don't you go getting sick on us, Ted-D. If I am coming down with something, we will need you to take care of things."

"I won't get sick, Alec. I'm here for you. One for all and all for ---" Ted-D was interrupted by Alec's coughing. "You get better big sister. We need you."

"I will do my best. As we know, like that book Daddy used to read many years ago, being sick is no fun."

"That it isn't." Ted-D ran off only to return with a blanket for Alec. "Here you go. Now, you get your rest while I make sure all is taken care of around here. Don't you worry about anything."

"Thank you, Ted-D. You have really become a big boy. And a big helper. I am so proud that you are my brother."

Ted-D beamed a smile that lit up the room, then he left to make sure all was good around the house so as Alec would not have to worry about a thing.

***

Summer passed quickly that year, leaving in its path, this beautiful day to be working in the yard. Fall was in the air and the birds were eating at the feeders. Sun shining. Blue sky. Perfect. I began the day weed trimming and finalized the lawn with a shorter than usual mowing. Going in the house to get some homemade lemonade, I stopped in my footsteps at the entry to the kitchen. The smell of something that had been dead for quite some time met my nostrils. Did Alec find a dead mouse in the house. Unusual, but one never knows. Although I believe I would have smelled it sooner. Or maybe it just started to smell? I looked beneath the stove, even moving it from the wall, the refrigerator also. Nothing. I then smelled my arm pits. Thankfully it wasn't me. After a wee bit, the smell was gone. Maybe I had something on my shoes last time I walked in the room?

After pouring myself some lemonade I went into the living room and found Alec snoozing in her chair. I still had to pet her. How could I not? She purred at my touch.

At the supper table that night...

"Look at her, Honey. She just doesn't seem to be getting better." Gloria and I were in the kitchen having dinner when Alec came in, took a paw, lifted one of her favorite toys and simply put it down. "It's like she isn't interested in much anymore. And she hasn't spoken in quite some time. I'm worried."

"I know, so am I." I reached for another chicken leg. "I'm just not sure with this Covid stuff going around. I really believe that it is affecting the pets too."

"I know. But I haven't seen too much on the news or the internet about Covid and animals."

"There is so much we don't know about it, yet all we can do is make sure she gets her rest, eats, and drinks. You know how much it put me down when I got Covid. I didn't do much for almost two weeks and then it took a few more to get back to par."

"That's true, Honey. I was scared for you then, too." Getting up for more milk, Gloria turned back towards me. "If only she could talk with us. I don't understand that part." She looked at Alec with so much love in her eyes. "Poor girl." She bent down to pet Alec. "You'll get better. I just know it. Time."

Alec looked up at Gloria and rubbed the side of her face in Gloria's palm. You could see the attachment between the two of them. The love was strong. I was hoping it would be strong enough to bring good health back to our girl.

Gloria looked up at me and said, "I helped her eat again this morning. She doesn't seem to mind when we do that. Although I get worried she may choke when we hold the bowls at an angle, that the food might slide into her too fast."

"I don't think we have to worry about that, Love. She does seem to know what is going on and if the food would do that, I am sure she would close her mouth or at least turn her face away."

"I suppose you are right. Even though she seems lethargic at times, she still has her wits enough to be safe. Maybe she is lethargic because of the meds from the vet?" Looking at Alec, Gloria shared that Alec did seem to like the new fish and shrimp food that she had recently purchased for her. "I was hoping she was just getting sick of eating the same thing week after week. The food items she eats have not changed much. Hard food. Soft food. The usual three or so styles of soft food at that, too."

"I don't know what to say, Love. We are trying all we can to help her get better."

"Yes, we are. I just wish there were more we could do. Even with the results from the vet, there wasn't much found. Maybe she does have a form of Covid. I just don't know." Gloria petted Alec as she talked. "She did get sick again last night. Vomit was the color or her food, but all liquid, no food parts. That's why I thought I would try to feed her this morning. She needs to get her strength back."

I didn't have much to say. I knew the vet had found a lump by Alec's heart when they took X-rays. Yet, the vet didn't come right out and say that was causing the issues because all they could see was a 3 cm mass. They couldn't tell if it was cancer unless they did surgery. Surgery was a decided no. The reason held was that we were told the success rate on that type of surgery was low. Very low. That was when they gave us the meds for Alec to take.

Later that day, Alec and I were alone in the house since Gloria and Ted-D had gone to the store. I picked Alec up in my arms. That was a bad thing. I had cradled her as I would a baby, her back in the crook of my arm, but it hurt her. She left out a painful moan, a sound I never heard from her before. My heart breaking for her, I hurriedly changed position to where she was comfortable. Belly down, back up, coddled in my arms, petting her.

"Oh, my buddy. I am so sorry. I didn't mean to hurt you." I thought I was going to start crying; I would never hurt Alec.

She looked up at me as though she understood. Then, she purred, a sign to show that she truly understood what I was saying.

Between my forefinger and thumb, I rubbed her ear. As I did so, she squinted her eyes in happiness, taking it all in.

"You mean the world to me, Alec. I only want the best for you and..." I couldn't believe what I was about to say. "And if it is time for you to leave this world, then you must. But I prefer you to stay. I know, I know. I am selfish in this way. I love you so much, as does Momma and Ted-D and Kayla Kitten. But I, we, don't want you to suffer any longer if you aren't going to get better." By now my eyes were blurry from the tears that broke their dam.

Again, Alec looked at me as if she understood all I had said.

"Let's take a walk around the house and visit your spots. OK, Alec?"

With that, Alec cradled in my arms, we took a tour of the house. We began by visiting Billie, her sheepskin rug she liked to lay on, all cuddled up and dreamy. I bent over so Alec could take her paw and pet Billie. "She is soft, isn't she, Alec?" Alec looked at Billie as if she yearned for better days of the past. I hugged her. I hugged her deep within my arms, close to my chest. Oh, how I hugged her. I did not want to let her go.

Giving Billie a pet myself, we continued into the other rooms of the house. Pausing by each of her favorite boxes, I recalled how she had been recently quietly escaping to a certain box that was by her tower of power in the living room, almost as if she was hiding. Very unusual I thought.

As we went room to room, she took everything in with a deep, thoughtful gaze. We both did. We finished with looking out the back window of the door of her room and then I knelt down by her food and water bowls. She slowly got out of my arms and laid by her bowls. I laid on the floor next to her.

The memories of how we used to sit and talk together, the belly and ear rubs gratefully given and received, all good times. We were both afraid we knew what was taking place here and now. And yet we tried to deceive our knowledge in accepting the fact.

***

Monday morning found me in a rush for an appointment. Barely enough time to shower, I got out of bed and straight to the bathroom to get ready for the day. Ted-D stayed sleeping.

With the morning ritual of brushing, flushing, and scrubbing complete, I opened the door of the bathroom to find Alec half lying down on the floor, sort of leaning against the hall wall. She looked up at me with horror in her eyes. A scared, helpless, horror. As if she had a stroke, she couldn't move as she should. I knelt on one knee and caressed her side. I felt her pain as if it were my own.

"What happened, Alec?"

She looked up at me, dazed and confused.

Hoping against the odds after all which had been happening of late, I asked if she had fallen from her tower of power. Again, she looked at me but said nothing. If only I had gotten up earlier, I would have had time to go in to see her before my shower. Oh my God, what if she was in pain, looking out her room, pleading for help and I had just walked past without a nod? Damn it all, Don! I caressed her side again. "I'll call Momma. OK, Alec?" I was at a loss of what to do.

Knowing that Gloria could not be disturbed with a phone call, I instead texted her. Then texted her again after I had not heard a reply.

Alec is not doing well. Looks like she had a stroke. I don't know what to do. Answer quickly, please.

I left Alec there on the floor, explaining to her that I was going to get dressed then I would be right back. She looked up at me as if she did understand that. That was good. If Gloria told me to take Alec directly to the vet, I would be ready.

I went down the hall to the bedroom and before I got my pants on, Alec walked in as if all was OK. She still did not talk, but she had lost that dazed, confused, scared look in her eyes. She seemed fine. Now, I was at a loss. I texted Gloria again, stating what was taking place at this moment and that since all seemed fine, I was going to go to my appointment. Five minutes later I was on the road heading west.

No sooner than I got on the big road, Gloria called me. I tapped the button on the steering wheel to answer the phone. "Hi."

"Where are you?"

"I just got on the highway. Alec seemed fine when I left, but I am still very worried. I don't know what to do."

Gloria replied, "I thought if you were home, that you could take her to the vet. I already made an appointment."

"I can turn around. I'm closing in on an exit ramp now."

"No. That's OK. I'll take off work. You go to your appointment, and I'll let you know what is going on when I know."

"OK. I hope all is well. I am so scared for her right now. I do not know what to do."

You could hear the sadness in Gloria's voice when she replied, "Me too. I love you."

"I love you, too." The phone went silent. And to myself I thought, "Damn it all, why does life have to be so busy for us? I should be home with my buddy, taking care of her."

Three hours later, I got the text message from Gloria.

The vet states they will need to take some tests. Blood work, etc. Alec needs to stay overnight. That's all I know for now. Love you.

An hour later, when I left for work, as always, just before I closed the door to leave, I yelled back into the house, "I love you, Ted-D. I love you, Alec." That's when it dawned on me. Alec was not home. My heart broke. She has to be OK. I yelled back to Ted-D. "Everything will be alright, buddy. Alec will be home tomorrow." I heard Ted-D stifle a whimper and answer, "I know Daddy. Alec will be OK. She's my big sister. She must be OK."

That night when I got home, instead of going directly into the house, I walked into the backyard. Looking up at the night sky, I saw Orion. In my life, Orion has always followed me wherever I had been. Good times. Bad times. East coast. Down south. All over. Orion had been above me, looking down and giving me energy to continue. No matter what I was going through. Tonight, he was watching over me again.

I looked up into the brisk, clear sky, the stars glittering their pattern as sands on a beach with a winter's frost. "You know I need her. You know I love that cat like I never would have thought. Now, this?!?!? I know we don't live forever down here, but this sucks." I paused a moment, took a deep breath, and continued, "Yet, I don't want to see Alec suffer. If you really need to take her, please do it before she suffers any longer. And, if you do take her, you better frickin' take good care of her or you'll have me to answer to when I arrive."

As soon as I said those words, a shooting star, coming from behind my right shoulder, slit through the darkness. "I'll take that as a sign you will take care of her *if* she needs to return home." I wiped the tears from my eyes and went inside. I sure hope Gloria and Ted-D are holding up better than me.

***

"She's home and eating some." It was Gloria calling me at the office. "We have to take Alec back in again tomorrow, 1:00 p.m. is the ultrasound."

"OK, Love. How long does the ultrasound take?"

"They told me she would have to stay a few hours."

I could feel the pain grow inside me at these words. I was already missing her. "A few hours? OK. Not much we can do to speed them up. It all takes time. How is she doing today?"

"She's drinking water, so at least she is staying hydrated. But now she is just lying next to her water dish."

"It sounds like the poor girl is exhausted. I'm glad to hear that she drank some water though. Still..." my voice drifted into silence.

"Yes, I'm keeping a close eye on her just in case anything else happens."

"Understood. Now, I take it they do the ultrasound right there at the vet?"

"Yes. That is correct."

"Should I take the day off tomorrow?" In my mind I am thinking, say yes. I really need to be with my buddy.

There was a brief silence and then Gloria responded. "I asked Alec if she would like that, and she looked as if she nodded yes."

"OK then. I will stay home tomorrow and join my buddy and you to go to the vet. Anything else?"

"Yes," Gloria replied, now with a frightened tone in her voice. "They say there is a tumor in front of her heart that could be cancer. But doing the x-ray they can only see the mass. With the ultrasound they hope to be able to see it better. They gave her steroids today and took blood work to see if there is anything that shows in that."

In attempts at a calm, positive reply I mentally slowed my talking down. "Well, it sounds like they are covering all bases." I was also hoping it was only a fatty mass and no cancer.

"Yes, they are. Other than that, nothing else to report."

"Well, I appreciate you keeping a close eye on her. I'm sure Ted-D is helping too. As for Alec, I sure hope it's as simple as she ate something she should not have and that it will soon pass."

"Yes, me too. Yes, Ted-D is a big help. I am so glad of that."

"Well, I will let you go then. And to double check, I should take tomorrow off?"

"Unless you would like to come home now. It would be nice if you were here with us. It's not like Alec to lay by her water bowl like this."

"In that case, I'll see you soon. I'm shutting down the computer in two minutes. See you in twenty."

"Thanks, Honey. See you soon. Love you."

"Love you, too."

That night, the three of us – Gloria, I, and Ted-D – kept Alec company. We made sure she was comfortable and petted. A lot. She seemed to be out of breath, and we were beginning to wonder about the mass that was against her heart. Maybe that was adding pressure and not allowing the heart to beat as it should?

The following morning, Gloria left for work while Ted-D and I slept a couple more hours. We usually woke up to Alec sleeping by my pillow or pressed against my leg, her hair in my nose. Thankfully, we were surprised to see she indeed got up in bed with us, so we cuddled for about a half hour before Alec decided that was enough. Ted-D and I were elated.

Later, after we got up, we walked into Alec's room, and we noticed she was in her tower of power's nest area washing her face.

"Well, this is a great surprise, Alec," I said. "It's great to see you up and about. You have made my day."

"Mine too, big sister," added Ted-D. "Are you feeling better?"

Alec looked at Ted-D and I but didn't say a word. Instead, she smiled at us. We were thrilled with that. She really looked great and that made all of us happy.

I texted Gloria to let her know the good news and that Alec was now taking a nap. I thought this would let Gloria have a better morning, knowing Alec seemed a lot better. It did.

At 12:45 p.m. Alec and I met Gloria at the vet for Alec's ultrasound. Since Alec was going to be there for a couple of hours and the results would not be known for a few days, we decided that

Gloria would pick Alec up on her way home from work.

***

The following afternoon I found that Alec had over-shot her litter box while urinating. My heart sank. This was not like her. Things were not pointing in the right direction, and I didn't like it. I'm sure she didn't either. She sat nearby and listened to me.

"Not a good time in the litter box today I see. That's OK. Things happen." I tried to sound positive and not let my worries show. "I'll get this cleaned up and everything will be good. Don't worry about it buddy." I bent down to pet her. "I love you. You are the best." And with that I gave her a hug.

I cleaned up the floor and took the mat outside to hose down, hanging it over the garden gate to dry. Back inside it was nice to see Alec enjoying the sun.

She looked good as new again. She even ate and drank like nothing was wrong. Maybe, hopefully, she was on the mend.

***

Gloria called me during her lunch break to check on Alec and to see if we needed anything at the store.

"Do we need some more suet for the birdies?"

"Ya. That's a good idea. They do like their suet. Just make sure it's the non-melt."

"For sure. OK, I'll see you when I get home."

***

"Hi Love. How was shopping?" I walked out to her van to help carry in the groceries.

"It was crowded, but not too bad. How is Alec doing?"

Grabbing bag five onto my wrist I told her about Alec overshooting the litter box but then how she seemed to be better after that. "I did hang the mat over the garden gate. Figured it could dry out better that way after I cleaned it up with the hose."

"Thanks for taking care of that. Did she eat?" Gloria carried the soda, a case in each hand, behind me.

"She did eat a bit and drank good. I am so proud of her." I opened the door. "Oh, there she is now."

I had just opened the door when I spotted Alec waiting at the threshold. Unlike the past, today she attempted to go outside. "No, no buddy. You know better than that." I took my foot and guided her back into the house.

"That wasn't like her at all." Gloria stated as she put the soda down on the kitchen table. Looking down at Alec we noticed her gaze seemed fixed to the outside world. The sun was low in the sky.

"No, she's never done that before. I think from now on we better make sure she is in her room before we unload the groceries." Gloria nodded in agreement. "We don't need her getting lost or run over by a car."

"Well, since she's in here, I'll go vacuum her area; didn't want to disturb her when she was in there enjoying the sun."

"OK, Honey. I'll take care of putting things away." Gloria knelt to pet Alec; I went to clean up her room. Behind me, I could hear Gloria talking with Alec, "I've been so worried about you today..."

I called Gloria from work that night. I did not know it before going in but my coworker on the next shift was not going to be there tonight, so that meant I'd be staying later.

"Just an fyi, Love, I will be here until 1:30. Dan's not coming in tonight."

"OK. Thanks for letting me know. I'll make sure the door is locked."

"How is Alec doing?"

"She was laying by her bowls for a long time, then I got her some fresh water and food. She ate a little after that."

"Oh, that is so good to hear."

"Yes, now she is laying in her box by the tower of power. She seems good."

"So glad to hear that, Love. How is Ted-D doing?"

"He's watching out the front window with Timone. You know, the stuffed animal we got the other week."

"Oh, yes. He sure likes him. I'm sure he'll sleep good tonight, keeping you and everyone safe today."

"I am sure of it. I just hope he doesn't start snoring. I know I can be loud just by myself." Gloria laughed at her wit.

"So true. The other night it was so peaceful in the bedroom I got scared. I am so used to you snoring I had to check if you were breathing."

"Smarty pants. By the way, I plan on getting to sleep sooner tonight. Staying up late for the past few nights has taken its toll on me."

"I can understand that. Not sure how you do it. I can't anymore. Wish I could though. So much to do, not enough time."

"Oh, Wayne called so I went up there to help him; wrote out a few checks and helped him get channel four in on his TV. Oh, and he says hi."

"Well, I hope you tell him I say hi, too. He's cool." Smiling with my eyes, I added, "Wish I had more time so as to visit with him a bit more. You know, watch a few westerns and Packer games together."

"I know what you mean. One day. One day soon."

"I sure hope so. Well, I best get to work. Love you, Love."

"Yes, and I better get the wash done. See you when you get home. Love you, too. Awe! I just heard Alec purr."

Although we were on the phone, I could sense Gloria's face break out into the largest smile within Ma Bell. I know I did.

The next day a friend of mine, Brenda, from band messaged me asking how Alec was doing. I was happy to let her know that Alec had helped me make the bed that day. I then sent her a photo of Alec with Billie, followed up with a photo of Alec with Ted-D. Brenda replied with a smile gif and stated that made her day. I thought her to be so kind to have asked. None of Gloria's or my family seemed to care. N'er a mention. Except for Wayne. Again. He is so cool.

***

"Omg awesome! Did she get up there herself?" Gloria stood by our bedroom door, looking in on Alec. Laying on our bed, Alec returned the look.

"Yes. She decided she and Billie needed to take a nap together." I put my arm around Gloria and like two proud parents, we beamed. Not only that but Ted-D joined in too. "That's my big sister," he boasted. Our hearts melted.

***

Over the course of the next few days, I kept myself busy scouring the internet for anything that might tell us what we could do for Alec, to make her all better. For whatever reason, my fixation was on cat constipation. I don't know why, especially since Gloria stated the fact that Alec could not have a bowel movement unless she had something to get rid of. It was as if my mind glossed over that fact since I did not know where else to look for an answer. The vet didn't give us much. So? Alec must have some form of Covid? Inside I was going insane. I had to help my little buddy get better.

Meanwhile, Gloria was doing all she could to help our little buddy, too.

"Hi Honey, how did practice go?" I had just walked in from another two-hour practice session with my sax professor.

"Went well. Learning a lot of great stuff that I never gave a thought to. Jazz music is a whole different lion." I put the saxophone case down on the floor and the music on the counter. "How are you doing?"

Gloria shrugged her shoulders and replied, "I'm doing OK. Kayla came over for a little visit. She said she wanted to spend some time with Alec, you know, just in case."

I looked at the floor when she said those words but agreed. "That was very nice of her. How is Sir, her kitten, doing?"

"He's doing well. Sir doesn't care much for her other cats, but he is behaving. Well," she paused, then laughed as her eyes sparkled. "the best Sir can."

"He is a big fur ball, isn't he?" I smiled, then heard a bit of a squeak. Walking into the living room I saw Alec was lying in her box. She looked up at me and attempted to smile.

"Poor girl has been there since you left. She did get up for a bit and went to her food dishes, but she didn't eat."

"She really does need food in her, don't you think?"

"Well, that is why I fed her by hand today. She had taken some soft food from me. She also had some licks of the fresh fish stuff I had in her dish. That treat stuff I picked up the other day in hopes of her maybe eating something?"

"Yes. I remember. I'm glad you got that. Every little bit helps." I laid next to the box Alec was in and began stroking her fur. She seemed to like that; I know I did.

Gloria continued, "She's urinated but no bowel movement. But she must have something in her bowels to have a bowel movement. She's been mostly drinking her food. And basically, we just started to hand feed her last night with the soft food."

"That's true," I agreed. "We are trying everything within our power to make sure she gets better."

"I hope this works, Don. That this soft food works its way into her bowels so she can eliminate it."

"Before I left this morning, she did eat rather well. I was surprised at how much she ate." I swallowed hard, looking up at Gloria, I uttered, "We can't lose her."

"No, we can't. But..."

"I know, I know." I didn't want to admit to it. I didn't want to know. But I did. "I know. It's out of our hands." I took a deep breath. "But I am not giving up."

Gloria agreed, "None of us are giving up."

From behind us, we heard Ted-D whimpering. Turning around we saw him wipe the tears from his fur as he stated, "I am not giving up on my big sister either." And then he stomped his foot in determination. "We will do our best to make sure Alec gets better."

"Yes, we will." Gloria and I agreed. And then we stomped our feet, too. Even with a dazed look in her eyes, Alec looked happy at what she just witnessed.

***

That evening I called Gloria into the office. She came in and took a seat as I began reading from the computer monitor, "How much pumpkin do you give a cat? When it comes to constipation or diarrhea, not much. For a small cat begin with a half teaspoon and continue up to two teaspoons if needed. It doesn't take much to begin working."

"I don't think she has constipation." Gloria paused, thought a bit and continued, "I think she is empty, and we need to fill her up. We can see about giving her some pumpkin tonight. I just don't want to give her diarrhea."

"That sounds good, Hot Lips." I joked with Gloria. She smiled. "You're one heck of a nurse."

"Thanks, Honey." She came over and hugged me around the neck. "I am so scared."

"Me too." I spoke. "Me too."

Gloria didn't get to the door to leave the office when I added, "One more thing. It says on this other page that some cats have round pupils because it is a side effect of the medication they are on."

I could hear Gloria's voice break as she went down the hall. "Good to know. Thanks for sharing."

Alec kept her place in her box, curled up in a soft blanket while I went back to more writing. She seemed to be resting well and I was so thankful of that.

Getting up to stretch my legs, I decided to take a stroll in the back yard. The sun had been traded for the moon by this time and I left out a bit of a gasp when I noticed this upon opening the back door. As Alec would attest, I do lose myself in my writing and time escapes my being without my noticing.

It was that time where the bats replaced the birds, soaring about in the blackness in attempts of a meal on wings. It was nice to see that they had returned. My hope was that they would get larger in their population in our area now that I put up that big bat house. It worried me as the "White-nose syndrome" was closing in upon our section of the United States.

I sat down on one of the back benches and looked up at the stars that were beginning to break the black curtain. By the looks of things, it was going to be a clear night. I leaned my head back to stare up at Orion, deep in my thoughts. When I opened them, a drone appeared over the house. Odd. First time I had seen a drone at night. Here or anywhere. Within a matter of seconds, it was gone in what appeared to be a magical trick. "Well, that was quick," I thought as I got up. "I'll have to look into nighttime flying since there does not seem to be enough time during the days."

***

"Alec ate really good this morning." I was so excited to tell Gloria that, that I didn't even wait for her to say good morning.

"That is so good to hear." She bent down to give Alec a pet.

"I also took her for a tour of our house."

"A tour?"

"Yup." I smiled. "I carried her to each room and talked about all we did or saw in each room. Trying to give her a reason to move about a bit more."

"That's an interesting way to give her motivation." She smiled at my crazy idea.

"I know, I know. But I am pulling everything out trying to help her get healthy. She had some water too. On her own."

"She does look good this morning. Maybe she had a good night's rest. It has been a while; I am sure since she has. It must be nerve-wracking for her."

"I would think so, too. Oh," my voice got softer, "she did have a little puddle outside her litter box again. Not much, but all the same."

Alec looked up at me as if she was asking why I had to tell her momma about this.

"Alec, if we keep communicating, if we all know what's going on, we can get you back to health as soon as possible."

Alec curled up at my feet. She understood. I got down to her level and petted her on her back, then gave her a belly rub. She purred. She purred! She sure knew how to make her momma and daddy happy.

Ted-D ran into the kitchen. "Did my big sister let out a purr?" Ted-D asked with glee in his voice.

"Yes, she did." Gloria and I answered him in unison. Ted-D dove into Alec and gave her a big hug. Then Ted-D listened to Alec's chest as she purred for him.

"More pumpkin tonight?" I asked Gloria.

"Yes. Maybe it is working. We'll keep it up for the time being." We walked into the living room, leaving Ted-D and his big sister Alec to some nice alone time together.

Gloria turned to me and said, "It kind of worries me with Alec going outside her litter box. I don't think she means too. I know she's sick. But it worries me."

"I understand. I'm worried myself, but we need to keep positive for Alec."

"Ted-D too."

"For sure."

"I left her litter rug outside for now. It makes cleaning up after her easier. At least until we know she is getting better; I think we will just keep it outside."

"Good idea," I agreed.

The next morning, we found some hope as in a wee bit of poop. Alec didn't make it to the litter box, but close to it.

"Yay, poop!" Gloria exclaimed.

The rest of the day went uneventful, as Alec spent most of it in her box, the one she rescued from the recycling after Christmas. The one from Kayla Kitten.

Alec had gone to the bathroom a couple of times, but no more bowel movement. At least she made it inside her litter box. You could tell that made her feel better too. She was never one to make a mess before.

"I'm beginning to think she has problems with either her lower back or pelvis area. Maybe she had fallen or tripped?"

"It is possible that she may have fallen and hurt herself," Gloria replied.

"Ted-D and I am hoping so and that she will be back on the mend soon." I slowed myself down. She was in a lot of pain this morning when I picked her up, so I didn't want to get my hopes up. That was just before she went to urinate. I don't think I'll have her in my arms when she lays on her back. It wasn't good. Poor girl. Too much curve in her spine when I cradle her like that."

"No, best to not hold her like that," Gloria said. "Oh, to let you know, I thought we would try something a bit different when we feed her."

"OK. What are you thinking?"

"I thought we could cut her food in squares while it's still in the can. Then we can give her a square every couple of hours to avoid psyching her out. Mind over matter or whatever you want to think of it as."

"Worth a try."

"She needs solid food to poop and to give her strength. Without her eating right she is weak. And when we are weak it's hard to do anything."

"You got that right."

"She is trying, so we aren't going to quit trying either."

"We're fighters. We don't give up."

"No, we don't." It was Ted-D from the other room. Ted-D bounded into the room to join us. "Should we add a pinch of pumpkin over the squares of food for Alec, too? I recall Daddy and I reading that cat food does not contain enough fiber." Ted-D looked up at Momma with wide eyes.

"That sounds like a very good idea, Ted-D," Momma answered.

That day, Alec's breathing went from bad to very well and she rested nicely. Don messaged Gloria before he left for work:

Leaving for work soon but wanted to let you know how the day progressed. Her breathing is very good now, but this morning when I took her into her room by her food it was not well. It was bad. She got out of my arms and laid on her side, her chest heaving, her mouth open, her paw outstretched trying to scratch the wall. I laid down on the floor with her and held her paw, I thought she was leaving. Strange -NEAT- thing was as I went to write this for you, she got up and went to pee. She is a fighter. I just wish we knew what was wrong. Yet, I am beginning to think she hurt herself the other morning while I was in the shower. Remember, she was in the hall and her one side was wobbly and then she laid down on the floor? It is just strange how her back side is by her haunches when

she is laying on her belly. It just seems too thin in that area.

Gloria messaged back:

Yes, I do remember. Yes, let her rest. It's thin because she is losing muscle mass. Without her eating, her body is taking it from other parts of her body. Being only 8 lbs., it doesn't take much. Since she's losing it in that area it's probably painful too. It's like she's all bones.

Don:

Thanks, Love. I'll leave her sleep, Ted-D is by his stuffed friend, Blue, waiting for you to come home. Carey is working from home today so she should be ready to go to band practice, I hope I am. I'll leave about 4:50 to go by her and pick her up. For now, I'll mow the lawn and take care of the birdies. Love you, Love. {{}}

Gloria:

Love you honey. If I don't see you before you go. Have a good time at band.

Don:

OK. I will do my best. Love you, Love.

Sep 1, 2021, 10:07 AM

Don:

Love you

Sep 1, 2021, 10:26 AM

Gloria:

Thank you honey. Love you.

Don:

You are welcome love. They are cuddling really nice. I even opened the front door for some fresh air for them. Love you.

Gloria:

Did you set her up there?

Don:

Nope. She was enjoying it there when Ted-D and I got up.

Big smile inserted here.

Gloria:

That is wonderful.

Love you.

Don:

Love you love

Sep 1, 2021, 12:27 PM

Don:

Ted-D photo bombed Alec

Gloria:

Oh Ted-D!!! Alec's eyes look normal.

Don:

Lol I know. Ted-D loves his big sister. I was hoping you would notice her pupils, too. I think the same thing. She ate and drank some again. I think she needs her rest, but she knows better than us in that area.

Gloria:

That is so good that she is doing better. Glad to hear she got up there by herself. I'm sure Ted-D will take good care of his sister, too.

Don:

Yes, for sure. I have her set up for when I have to go to work. Ted-D is also going to sit with her.

Gloria:

Oh wow!!!

Don:

Glad you approve. We try. Love you love. I need to feed the birds now. Didn't know it was so late. Love you love. Hope your day is going good.

Gloria:

Day is good. Love you honey!! You too!!!

Sep 1, 2021, 3:17 PM

Don:

FYI: I put fresh, out of the tap, water in her bowl. She did drink some while I held the bowl for her before I left. Love you, Love.

Since bottled water lacks in a lot of different things that tap water does, maybe giving her bottled water was the wrong thing to do? I don't know. Love you, Love.

Gloria:

We will continue with tap for now. It's so hard to know. We are doing all we can. Thank you honey. Love you.

Sep 1, 2021, 4:24 PM

Don:

Something I found. Just an fyi for you, Love. Love you! The general consensus of my research is distilled water is NOT recommended. Although most electrolytes and minerals important for good health are found in all commercially prepared dog and cat foods; many pets do not get balanced diets. Drinking regular water is not only important for proper hydration but is also a source for these necessary minerals and electrolytes that your pet might not get if he/she is a finicky eater. Remember, always provide ample fresh drinking water for your pets daily, the same water that you drink.

Gloria:

That is good information honey. Thank you. It doesn't seem she moved much. But she is resting.

Love you honey

Don:

Thanks for the update, Love. Every now and then she would lie further down on the couch but when I would be in the house, she would move back to where you see her now. She is sneaky, too. Love you, Love. Hoping she has a better night.

Gloria:

There is nothing in her litter box yet.

She's such a good girl.

Don:

Yes, Alec is sooooo good. I can't wait til she is back to feeling good again.

Gloria:

She's doing her best

Don:

Yes, she is. Hi to Alec and Ted-D for me.

Gloria:

They say hi!!

Sep 1, 2021, 9:53 PM

Don:

FYI Love. Love you. 1) What can I give my cat to stimulate her appetite? Try catnip. Some cat owners have said that catnip has stimulated their cat's appetite. It's

worth a try, as it can't harm them, and it can be a form of enrichment.

2) 8 pounds kitty can also take 2.5 (5 drops) - 5 mg CBD once or twice a day. Always start at the lesser amount. CBD can help with pain and also stimulate a kitties hunger.

Love you, Love.

Gloria:

Is the stuff you have the right stuff CBD

Don:

Basically yes. They were talking about human CBD.

As long as it doesn't have any coconut or other plant oils in it.

Gloria:

Ok we will try both of those things. We have to make sure on that.

Don:

Because kitties are carnivorous.

Gloria:

Oh boy. She hasn't gone potty but she did drink water.

Don:

Can you give cats human CBD oil? Although there have been no studies, a vet says that CBD oil is generally safe for cats. So, this is good. Water is the most important. But if we can get her to start eating her foods, that would be a big step.

Gloria:

I know.

Don:

How is she doing otherwise.

Gloria:

> **She's having a hard time breathing.**
>
> **She keeps stretching out.**

Don:

Sounds like something is pinched? Maybe the CBD can help? I don't know. But that is what I had read...

Gloria:

It could be. We should try the CBD.

Don:

> **OK. We shall. These guys say it does wonders....**

Gloria:

> **And catnip**

Don:

OK. Catnip too. If anything, it may make her more comfortable in her last stage with us. Another article written was about this very deal where their kitty was suffering for a month. CBD helped it relax.

Gloria:

I forgot my blood pressure medication this morning and my nerves, anxiety, and bp are pretty whacked. I took it when I got home tho. Took BP and it's 128/90. Love you honey.

Don:

We don't need anything happening to you, My Love. Y-O-U are a big part of the nucleus. The energy expels from the center....

Gloria:

Ok. I'll let you be. Hurry home safely. I don't like being home alone with her. I worry. Sorry. I try to be positive tho!! Love you!

Don:

I'll be home asap. Hang in there, My Love. We are all energy. Positive gets positive. But sometimes, things are beyond our control. Still, until then, we will do our best to help Alec... Love you, Love. See you soon.

VIIII
The Energy

I arrived home at 10:52 p.m. Gloria met me at the door.

As I entered the house, Gloria wrapped her arms around me. "Don. I'm scared. She's on the couch but she is having problems breathing. It's been like this all night. I don't know what to do."

"I know. We are doing the best that we know how. All of us."

"Yes, Ted-D has been by Alec's side all night. He's doing his best to be a big, brave brother. He's scared though. I am too. I'm afraid Alec is not going to live much longer." Gloria shed a few tears. I held mine back, not too well though.

"Well, we must make sure she is comfortable. Let's go into the living room. We should make sure she gets her medicine." In my mind I am thinking how in the hell am I sounding so in charge. I am as scared as Gloria. I cannot, WE cannot lose our Alec buddy.

Upon entering the room, Ted-D turned from Alec and looked at me. When I got nearer, Ted-D jumped into my arms and whispered in my ear, "Daddy, Alec isn't doing too well. She is really sick, isn't she?"

"Yes, I'm afraid she is." My voice trembled.

Ted-D put his little arms around my neck. "I don't want to lose my big sister,

Daddy. Isn't there anything you can do?"

"I wish there was, Ted-D." I choked up but continued, "All we can do now is make sure Alec is comfortable."

"Don't cry, Daddy. My fur is getting wet."

"I'm sorry, Ted-D. It just hurts." I gave Ted-D a big hug.

"It's OK, Daddy. Hug away." And he gave me a big hug in return.

Gloria came from the kitchen. "Here's Alec's medicine."

Taking it from her outstretched hand, Gloria traded me the medicine for Ted-D. Ted-D hugged his momma tight, Gloria returning it to Ted-D.

I knelt by the couch where Alec was lying. She looked up at me with a distant look in her eyes.

"It's OK, Alec. You know what I have always said when this started." Alec continued to look at me, this time directly into my eyes as if she still understood what was taking place. "If it is your time to leave us for better places, then it is time. But my gosh, buddy, I don't want you to leave." I bent over and brought Alec to my chest. She made a noise as if in pain and I backed my hug off. "Let us get you your medicine now, OK?" I picked Alec up and together, Gloria, I and Ted-D decided it would be easier to give Alec her medicine on her tower of power so we could be eye-to-eye.

I handed the medicine to Gloria and gently put Alec up on a shelf of her tower of power. Alec lied down, exhausted. A more distant look in her eyes now. I held back my tears.

Gloria gave me the medicine bottle as Ted-D looked on in wonder. "Is this going to make Alec comfortable, Daddy?"

"That's what the vet tells us, Ted-D. It has seemed to be helping Alec a bit."

"That's true, Daddy. Alec did feel a bit better the other day when she took it. She even went up by Billie and cuddled with her for a while."

I took the medicine dropper and measured off a dose to give Alec. As I did so, Alec turned away from it, as if she had had enough. That was not like her, but, after a bit of coaching, she decided to take her medicine.

As soon as she took the medicine, she jumped up in the air to which I grabbed her so as to make sure she didn't fall to the floor. None of us knew what was taking place but Alec sprang from my hands. She ran for the litter box. We all stood back and watched the doings. Alec leapt into the litter. Dug a hole. And proceeded to go potty. Since she had not gone to the bathroom much all day, we were all overjoyed. Then she covered it up, and, with a burst of adrenaline, went for the back door that led to the yard. She was trembling.

The door was closed so she laid down on the mat, continuing to shake uncontrollably. Ted-D snuggled deeper into his momma's arms as Gloria stood back wide-eyed; none of us knew what was taking place. I knelt by Alec and started to pet her, slowly, running my fingers along her spine.

Alec looked at me in her frenzy and spoke for the first time in weeks. "Daddy, I'm scared. The energy. The energy. It is so strong. I need to release it, it hurts. It hurts, Daddy." She held out her left paw, it quivering beyond control. "Hold my paw, Daddy. I don't want to be alone. I'm scared."

I took Alec's paw in my hand and then laid down next to her, putting my head against her side, listening to her heart. It resonated such as a large bass drum. THUMP, THUMP, TH.

I held Alec's paw tighter, scared within the sound of silence. I listened closer. Nothing. I looked up at Gloria and Ted-D, each with fright in their eyes. I put my head against Alec's side again. Again, nothing. I felt the cold enter her empty, spiritless body. I turned my head towards Gloria and Ted-D. "She's gone."

You could see the hurt in their eyes. This was not supposed to happen. I was the fixer! And yet, here I was, my best friend gone. Gone to me. Gone to Gloria and Ted-D. Gone.

I got on one knee to pick Alec up, hugging her close to my being, my tears streaming down like an endless creek in flood season. I looked at Gloria and Ted-D, asking Gloria if she would like to hold Alec. She shook her head, no.

Bringing myself up on both feet now, with Alec clutched tightly to my chest, I walked the few steps to Gloria and Ted-D. I held Alec out a bit so they could touch Alec, pet Alec, talk with Alec as her spirit filled the tiny room. As I did, Alec's head fell out of the palm of my hand in which it was cradled. I didn't know if I was to laugh or cry out in horrific terror. Again, I was the fixer and here I was, with no way to fix this event except to re-cradle my four-legged buddy's head in my hand.

Gloria petted Alec, rubbing her ear as Ted-D knelt at his waist, still in Momma's arms, and reached out to stroke Alec's cheek.

"I'm going to miss you, big sister," Ted-D said in between sobs. "Thanks for being my big sister and teaching me so good. I'll always love you, Alec."

***

I didn't want her to die alone.

I wanted to be there.

I wanted to hold her paw.

I wanted her suffering to stop.

And now?

I wish I could bring her back.

I felt as if I had failed my dearest friend.

Alec passed at 11:15 p.m. that night.

We were all there with her.

***

I took my coffee out to the patio, deep in my thoughts of the book Alec and I was writing. A bee buzzed by and sounded like it said Daddy. If that wasn't the darndest thing. Still, it stung. The pain of missing Alec was still in me, even though it had been a month. It wasn't as bad, but it is nowhere lighter as I was hoping.

Inside the house, her cremains rest in a beautiful urn, her paw print cast in plaster, a lock of her hair beside it. Rubs was keeping watch. "No fear. Alec is safe."

The night prior I talked to Orion and asked about Alec, stating I'd like to have a sign that she was doing well. Nothing. Hours later, lying in bed, I felt a brush along my arm. I told myself it was nothing. But it was.

I still hear her paw steps in the hallway, even scratches upon the bathroom door. I see her in the window watching me work in the yard waiting for me to give her attention.

I miss her with a vengeance. Yet, I know that she is doing well in another realm, I really do. It's still painful not being able to hold her in my arms or have her sit on my shoulders so I could carry her to her tower of power. Her grand arrival of looking down upon the living room in an advantageous point that only she could do so eloquently. It hurts my soul as the pressure of a lava flow waiting to be released from within the inner depths of Mother Earth.

The other day I was uncovering Billie and Rubs near Alec's urn - Gloria covers them at night to keep them comfortable with Alec – and as I did so, I heard a purr. Alec had purred so loud from the other realm it was as if she was right there where I could see her. It was then that I felt that she was letting me know that all was good between her and me. That I did nothing wrong to cause her death. I was relieved, in awe, and missing her in my arms. But she left me know that all was good and that she was happy – content – and that her energy would always be around. She also let me know that she felt more than loved every time I made the bed and had the pillow moved as I always did, so as she could walk directly onto the bed instead of trying to get around the pillow.

Another night in bed, I felt a brush against the back of my head in an area where I still have hair. It was very similar to what I had felt a week before Alec's departure. That night, I thought – I hoped – that Alec had come up her stairs by the bed and was going to cuddle with me. She was nowhere to be seen. I even looked upon the floor to see if she had decided to sleep with Billie, but she was not there either. I equated the "brush" on my hair to be simply my hair being moved by a movement of my pillow, even though I had not moved to make that happen. Feeling "the brush" this night and knowing that I wouldn't see my little buddy when I turned over, I still deduced that it was Alec, saying, "I'm here, Daddy. Even though you can't see me. I'm here."

This morning, Ted-D was lying on Billie, a kitty decorated blanket covering him, one leg poking out, just like Momma Gloria. As he looked out the window, I heard him whimpering, his back toward me. I rubbed him on the shoulder and asked him what was on his mind. He stated, "I'm afraid I will forget my big sister."

As I heard him speak those words, I held my tears back. Alec's death has taken a toll upon us all.

Pay It Forward

November came, Thanksgiving already past, and Ted-D was exclaiming with glee, "Don't worry, Daddy. I will be a huge help. Alec taught me how to be a great big brother. I will always remember what she taught me and now I can help you and Momma." Today was a big day. We were headed up north to adopt four kitties.

Alec's death had taken a huge toll upon us. We felt with all she had given us, all she had taught us, it should not be left to the winds. Inside ourselves, we felt as if she had taught us all she had in order to help others in the future.

Today was that future. There were four sisters that needed a loving home. We got the call and we were on our way to meet them.

Gloria had gone to the big box store earlier in the week to get another pet carrier so as the little fur balls would be safe on their trip to their new home with us.

"I was going to get three more carriers, but the adoption place told me we could easily get two kittens in each carrier. I sure hope they're right."

Gloria sounded like a nervous mom waiting to give birth to her first child. Ted-D and I smiled.

"I'll make sure they are not scared when they go in their carriers, Momma. I will keep them company. Maybe even sing them a song."

"That is so nice of you, Ted-D."

"Alec made me feel at home when I first came to live with you and Daddy. I was scared, but Alec let me know there was no reason to be scared. There is no reason for my new sisters to be scared either." Ted-D sounded so grown up sitting there on the kitchen counter, waiting for us all to go pick up the kittens.

Granted, he looked a bit scared, but then again, we all were. I know I was, as I never had more than one pet at a time. Still, it seemed as if it were Alec's wish for us to be doing this today.

"How is my bow tie, Momma? Does it look good? It's not crooked, is it?" He sounded so worried yet looked so dapper.

"You look handsome there, Ted-D. The green of your bow tie goes great with the color of your fur."

"Thanks, Momma. I thought my red bow tie would be too flashy. What do you think, Daddy?"

"I think you made a fine choice. Definitely green for this very special occasion."

"Thanks Daddy. You and Momma look very nice, too. I think we will make a good impression upon my new sisters foster parents."

"I believe you to be correct, Ted-D." I smiled at his wisdom. "We try our best, don't we?"

The trip up north took us on familiar roads until we got to the big city of Appleton. A city we had been to many times prior to watch Broadway shows at the Performing Arts Center. It is a lovely venue where the three of us held season tickets. Once we got near though, we entered areas we had never been before. That made the trip a wee bit more interesting.

We did not want to be late for meeting the kittens or their foster parents, so we had decided to leave with plenty of time to eat near our destination. Thankfully, we found the "new-to-us" diner without missing our turns.

Even though we let Ted-D know all was safe where we were parked, he stated he wished to wait in the truck to make sure no one would take the pet carriers. He proceeded to sit on the dashboard and watch out the windshield as Gloria and I went into the diner. An hour later, after a delicious meal, we returned to find Ted-D still on watch, waving at us as we got near.

"Hurry up, Momma. Hurry up, Daddy. We don't want to be late."

"It's OK, Ted-D. We are going to be right on time. Daddy has it all figured out."

"What if Daddy makes a wrong turn, Momma?"

"I'll use the map thingy on my phone, OK Ted-D?"

"OK Daddy. OK. I just don't want to be late and then my new sisters might get worried that we forgot about picking them up today."

"We will be there with time to spare. Now, get safely seated and I'll get us going."

Ten minutes later and one wrong turn we arrived almost on time. OK, a few minutes late, but nothing too bad.

As we got out of the truck, Ted-D had issues trying to contain his excitement. He jumped into Momma's waiting arms.

"Do I look OK, Momma? Daddy? I won't scare them, will I?"

"Now, why would you scare them, Ted-D? Are you going to yell "Boo!" when we go in?" Daddy joked.

"No," Ted-D answered. Then he found himself laughing too. "I am just so nervous. I hope they like me."

"You are doing well, Ted-D." Momma said. "I believe we are all a bit nervous, aren't we, Daddy?"

"Yes, we are." I answered. "And I am sure that the kittens and their foster parents are also. So, we should just go up and ring the doorbell and get this going, ey?"

"OK!" Ted-D said. "Let's go, Momma."

"Right beside you, Ted-D." And with that we entered our new world hand-in-hand-in-paw.

The woman of the house answered the door, letting us in without having to take off our shoes and introducing herself. Her husband sat on the couch, TV on.

"Winston. Winston," she called for her husband. "These are the fine people who are going to adopt the kitties today."

Winston turned from the TV and said, "Welcome." Then he surprised us. Actually, they both surprised us.

Looking at Ted-D, Winston asked, "Let me guess, you are going to be these girls' big brother?"

Ted-D looked directly at Winston and stated with a smile, "Yes, sir."

"I am so glad to hear that. They are a handful to take care of, but lots of fun." Ted-D giggled.

Karen then made mention that yes, her and her husband could also hear Teddy Bears. They consider it somewhat of a bonus for fostering kitties and cats until they have a forever home. "We count our blessings in so many ways. This is one of them. To be able to hear what others do not." By this time, Ted-D had already crawled onto Winston's lap. They were both talking like they were old friends.

So followed the next half hour, the five of us getting to know one another. Eventually, Ted-D got down on the floor and began crawling towards the kitties. Eyeing each other up - the kitties and Ted-D - they began to slowly play a form of hide and go seek. The four kitties and Ted-D were playing, jumping to and froe. Four sets of eyes would look up at us, wide-eyed. Then they would hide under a chair, peering out from beneath the blanket that covered the seat. Then Ted-D would sneak up behind them and yell, "Boo!" When he did so, he looked at Daddy only to see Daddy smiling back at him.

"I believe they are all going to be fine," Karen, the lady of the house said softly, watching the sisters and their new brother get acquainted. "It is as if they were always together." She sounded relieved. "I always get worried when it is adoption time. We always want a good home for the kitties and cats to go live."

"Now, Karen, these people seem fine. The girls will be good, and Ted-D here will be a great asset to them getting used to their new home." Then Winston added, "It's nice they will have a big brother to protect them, too. Such little girls they are. I'm going to miss these four."

Karen put her arm around Winston. "It'll be fine." Karen looked at us. "We have done this for so many years, fostering kitties and cats until they find that forever home that they can call their own. Still, it hurts to see them leave. One does get attached." She wiped a tear from her cheek.

"They have found their forever home. We can't believe how lucky we are to have them to love." Gloria took my hand in hers. "Don't worry, we will send you pictures and cards at Christmas." Gloria shared a smile with Karen. "We can't thank you enough for caring for them as you have."

"It is our pleasure," Winston chimed in. "Now, Ted-D. You make sure they are well taken care of, OK?"

"I will, Sir." And with that, Ted-D put his paw out and shook Winston's hand. "Alec taught me how to be a great brother."

"And a very well-mannered one at that." Winston smiled as Ted-D seemed

222

to glow in admiration of the words Winston spoke.

"Thank you." And with a hug for Winston and Karen the seven of us headed towards home, the four kitties yet to be named, safely in their carriers, with Ted-D keeping a mindful eye on each.

Back on the big road, my mind began to remind me that we were not replacing Alec. There was no possible way of doing that. Each person or pet or Teddy Bear are their own being. Still, I had to remind myself to treat these little kittens based upon who they are and not who Alec was. I could only keep reminding myself that Alec, being as good as she was, is the reason we now had four kitties added to our family. Had Alec not been a good girl, I think we may have gotten a Pomeranian puppy instead. Maybe.

My thoughts were interrupted by some purring. Some mighty loud purring. Gloria and I looked back at the kitties, but Ted-D said they were sleeping. Well, until now. That's when it dawned on me, it was my phone. Yes, I still hear Alec purring, but it is only when my phone rings. I pushed the button on the dash to stop the call since I did not recognize the phone number and I was good with my car insurance and its warranty. For the duration of the ride, I enjoyed listening to Ted-D tend to his sisters and peering over at Gloria who had the biggest grin upon her face. This time, she seemed to beam. Still, in my ears, I heard Alec purring...

Once home, Ted-D woke his sisters up with excitement filling the air around us. "Get up sisters. Get up. We're home. We're home!" Ted-D jumped up and down, rubbing his paws upon his legs and yelling once again, "Sisters, we are home!"

Gloria and Ted-D took one of the carriers and I took the other. All of us parade to Alec's old room to do the ceremonial release of the kittens, with the door of the room closed to the rest of the house. We didn't need them to run off without first knowing where their litter box was.

"OK, Love? Ted-D? Kitties? Is everyone ready?"

The kitties looked up out of the holes of their carriers. Gloria and Ted-D were all smiles. The consensus was, "Yes, we are ready."

We each opened the carriers we held and watched as the kitties came out. Slowly. Sniffing the air, looking here and there. Everything being strange to them and not sure if it was safe for them. Until...

"This is your new home sisters." Ted-D boasted. "And this was my big sister's room." With that Ted-D bit his lip a bit then continued. "Alec is happy you are here. And so am I."

Ted-D got down on his knees and coaxed his new sisters out into the freedom of the room, which they did slowly, being convinced all was good for them to do so. Gloria and I just watched, not saying a word.

Ted-D gently herded all four kittens towards the alcove where the litter box was placed. "Let us show Daddy that you know where to go when you need to go pee-pee and poopy."

As each took a turn sniffing their new bathroom amenity, one of the kittens jumped in and proceeded to use it, no qualm about all of us there.

"See Daddy. My sisters know where to go potty. Momma did you see, too?"

"Yes, I did." Gloria said. "You are teaching them so well."

"I'm glad they are quick learners."

"So am I, Ted-D", Daddy said with a smile.

"Sisters, did you see the new food bowls and the water bowl, too?" Ted-D simply couldn't keep his excitement contained. He wanted to show them everything at once. It brought back memories of making new friends when I was young. Still, I interrupted Ted-D.

"Yes, Daddy. What is it?"

"I just want to let you know; you do not have to show them everything right now. Let them get used to one thing and then use that as a building block."

"That's a great idea, Daddy. That way they won't get all messed up."

"That's right, Ted-D. My smart boy, you are, you are."

"Just one thing."

"Yes, Ted-D?"

"Right now, I'm messed up."

"Why? What's wrong?" Momma asked.

"Well, there are two blondes, one grey, and one mixed color. And we don't have names for any one of them. How do we name them?"

"I don't know Ted-D. Momma, what do you think?" Daddy asked of Momma.

227

Ted-D looked up at Momma as did the kittens and Daddy.

"Well, we can name them something that we feel at this moment. That way we can tell them apart, but if we give them a new name, it needs to be soon so as they themselves don't get mixed up, too."

As time went on, names were decided on with only one change...

"Boo-Boo, Yogi, Marbles, and Nellie have a fondness for water when it comes out of a faucet. They enjoy laying in sinks or bathtubs and chasing each other around the house. They love their mousie toys and blue twirlers. They took over Alec-the-Cat's towers of power and they love Ted-D like they love catnip. But I suppose you all know that. Don't you?" I asked with a smile.

Sitting on the back of the couch near the bay window, with excitement in his voice, Ted-D exclaims, "Momma's home, Momma's home."

Looking down at the kitties in my lap I ask, "Did you hear that? Sounds like Ted-D sees Momma pulling into the driveway. Time to get up now."

Boo-Boo looks up at me, extending her legs, yawning, smiling, and . . . "Mew. Momma's home."

The magic begins...

In this story, drawn from life and imagination, you had learned that

Alec-the-Cat was not "Just a cat" nor just a big brother to Ted-D Bear.

She was my friend and teacher, but it didn't begin as such. I was a dog person. Specifically small dogs. Pomeranians were my favorite. Alec knew this coming into my life, but she didn't care. She was a cat. She knew better. Attaching her nails in my heart and covering me in feline hair, she became my friend.

Until my last book is written, she will adorn every copyright page that is related with Jumping Cat Publications.

To see photos of Alec, please go to www.AlecGould.com and choose the tab <ALEC>.

CPSIA information can be obtained
at www.ICGtesting.com
Printed in the USA
BVHW041538051222
653478BV00010B/24